C000284981

Praise for *Create Amazing*

"In *Create Amazing*, Greg Graves argues persuasively that employee ownership—done the right way, and for the right reasons—can be a catalytic force for economic prosperity and corporate endurance. Drawing upon deep, practical experience as CEO of an employee-owned company, he lays out the what, the why, and the how of sparking an ownership mindset with an ESOP. Leaders who seek to fill their companies with people passionately engaged in the business for a very long time would do well to consider what Graves has to teach."

—Jim Collins, author, *Good to Great*

"As *Create Amazing* makes clear, employee ownership has a rich history in our country—and a strong future. Greg Graves has given us a how-to manual for combining good politics and economic policy to reduce economic disparity and improve the financial well-being of our nation."

—Jerry Moran, United States Senator, Kansas

"How should we solve economic inequality? Greg Graves, former CEO of one of the most important employee-owned corporations in the United States suggests we encourage the employees to buy the most successful firms in the country using credit and tax incentives using the ESOP (Employee Stock Ownership Plan). This book is the story of how Burns & McDonnell employees did it, of the central role of leadership in employee-owned firms, of the wealth that the middle class can gain from owning corporate assets, and finally, of the central role employee ownership can play in achieving the American dream of economic liberty for all."

—Joseph Blasi, director, Institute for the Study of Employee Ownership and Profit Sharing, Rutgers University School of Management and Labor Relations

"Greg Graves's new book is a must-read for any business leader thinking about how to transition the company into an ownership structure that will build productivity, loyalty, profits, and employee financial security. From his thoughtful review of the socioeconomic origins of employee stock ownership plans to the practical, how-to guide offering step-by-step insights on creating the strongest possible employee ownership model, Graves's analysis pays homage to the millions of workers who now reap the benefits of American employee-ownership as well as the millions more who could be employee-owners. Companies need to know from their peers—those who have been as successful under an ESOP model as Burns & McDonnell has been—that making the leap to employee ownership pays off not only for their employees' retirement accounts, but through the cultural shifts that occur, also in shockingly low worker turnover rates, higher productivity per worker, profits that allow for long-term thinking and deep reinvestment, and unmitigated business success. I cannot recommend this book highly enough."

—Stephanie Silverman, CEO, Employee Owned S-Corporations of America

"Greg Graves's dynamic leadership of a highly successful large multinational employee-owned company provides him with a unique perspective of wealth building in America."

—Doug Girod, chancellor, the University of Kansas

"I have known Greg Graves, a respected leader among CEOs, for many years. Through this book, Greg offers a comprehensive blueprint for how to improve businesses through employee ownership. His practical ideas and civic-minded approach will redesign the workplace and reinvigorate the American economy."

—Stuart R. Bell, president, the University of Alabama

"Greg Graves is not a theoretician sitting in an ivory tower, but a leader who built an incredibly successful company based on a model of shared capitalism: an ESOP. *Create Amazing* tells you how to bring this competitive advantage to your own company."

—Stephen Smith, CEO, Employee Owned Amsted Industries

CREATE
AMAZING

CREATE AMAZING

Turning Your Employees into Owners for Explosive Growth

GREG GRAVES

Matt Holt Books
An Imprint of BenBella Books, Inc.
Dallas, TX

This book is designed to provide accurate and authoritative information about ESOPs. Neither the author nor the publisher is engaged in rendering legal, accounting, or other professional services by publishing this book. If any such assistance is required, the services of a qualified financial professional should be sought. The author and publisher will not be responsible for any liability, loss, or risk incurred as a result of the use and application of any information contained in this book.

Create Amazing copyright © 2021 by Greg Graves

All rights reserved. No part of this book may be used or reproduced in any manner whatsoever without written permission of the publisher, except in the case of brief quotations embodied in critical articles or reviews.

BenBella Books, Inc.
10440 N. Central Expressway
Suite 800
Dallas, TX 75231
benbellabooks.com
Send feedback to feedback@benbellabooks.com

BenBella is a federally registered trademark.
Matt Holt and logo are trademarks of BenBella Books, Inc.

Printed in the United States of America
10 9 8 7 6 5 4 3 2 1

Library of Congress Control Number: 2020054064
ISBN 9781953295002 (print)
ISBN 9781953295231 (electronic)

Cowriting and editing by Leeanne Seaver
Editing by Greg Brown
Copyediting by Elizabeth Degenhard
Proofreading by Lisa Story and
    Michael Fedison
Text design by Publishers' Design
    and Production Services, Inc.

Text composition by PerfecType,
    Nashville, TN
Cover design by Sarah Avinger
Author photo by Ellie Grace Photography
Printed by Lake Book Manufacturing
See additional image credits on page 207

Distributed to the trade by Two Rivers Distribution, an Ingram brand
www.tworiversdistribution.com

Special discounts for bulk sales are available.
Please contact bulkorders@benbellabooks.com.

All roads lead to Deanna

C O N T E N T S

FOREWORD

*C*reate *Amazing* is a book for this time. Anyone who cares about America should be reading it.

Our country faces an unprecedented group of challenges: an uncontrolled pandemic; a depressed economy; deep political divisions; and many who believe that the system on which much of our national and economic success has been built no longer works for them.

Greg Graves offers an insight into one answer to these challenges: employee ownership.

Greg doesn't offer this answer as an abstract theory. Instead, he shares his experience leading a highly successful company that shared its success and wealth with its employees through an Employee Stock Ownership Plan, or ESOP. It is an outstanding story.

I, too, have the privilege of leading a company that is 100 percent owned by its workers through an ESOP. I, too, can testify that when employees benefit not only from the fruits of their labor, but also as owners of capital, it changes the entire culture of a company. They have "skin in the game."

It also allows workers in tough Rust Belt manufacturing jobs—the kinds of jobs that many American companies have outsourced to Asia—to have work careers that allow them to own homes, raise families, and retire with dignity.

Greg doesn't pretend that building a great ESOP-owned company is easy. But what's great about this book is that Greg digs into the nuts and bolts of what needs to be done to build a great ESOP company. There are a lot of logistical and practical details on which Greg shares advice. But, more importantly, Greg delves into what really makes an employee-owned company work—selfless and dedicated leadership, the kind he demonstrated for years.

And he doesn't pretend that one size fits all. Greg and I have had great fun comparing our very different paths to building companies that have changed the lives of thousands. What troubles us both is that more haven't taken advantage of this structure. *Create Amazing* offers a chance for many others to explore this company-changing opportunity.

So what holds many back from taking the steps toward a structure that promotes economic success for all workers? This is one case in which we cannot blame the politicians. As the board chair of the Employee-Owned S Corporations of America (ESCA), I had the chance to work with leaders from Greg's company and other ESOP companies on Capitol Hill and with representatives of the executive branch. We found strong bipartisan support for employee ownership and ESOPs.

Not that there aren't opportunities for Washington and state governments to do more—certain changes in legislation, regulation, and the offering of direct incentives could help promote ESOPs. There is huge opportunity right now. As the baby boomer generation passes businesses on to the next generation, we should be doing all we can to make sure they consider and have incentives to encourage transitioning those businesses on to their employees.

But what is also needed are leaders who are willing to put their egos aside and forgo ringing the bell at the NYSE in order to lead a company that gives its workers the opportunity to earn—earn, not be given—a share of the company. Greg and I can tell you that there is nothing more rewarding. For those who have the courage to do so, this book will start you on that journey.

I urge you, read Greg's book and create amazing.

—Stephen R. Smith, Chairman, President, and CEO, Amsted Industries

Amsted Industries is a 120-year-old, Chicago-headquartered company with more than sixty facilities and nearly 18,000 employees around the world. It is a leading supplier to the rail, vehicular, and industrial industries. Steve Smith has been CEO since 2017. He came to Amsted as president of Amsted Rail in 2005, and then spent time as vice president and general counsel. He is a graduate of Wheaton College (Illinois) and the University of Chicago Law School, and he completed the Advanced Management Program at the University of Michigan. Steve serves as a member of the Executive Committee of the Manufacturers' Alliance Board of Trustees, and is former board chair of the Employee-Owned S Corporations of America. In the community, Steve serves as board chair of Chicago's Grant Park Music Festival, as well as a member of the Economic Club of Chicago, the Commercial Club of Chicago, and the Board of Governors of the Chicago Symphony Orchestra. He is a former member of the Wheaton College Board of Visitors, the Visiting Committee of the University of Chicago Law School, and the Board of Elders of Immanuel Presbyterian Church.

INTRODUCTION

I Immediately Knew That the Most
Important Question Was "Why?"

Do you ever wake up from a good dream and try in vain to hold on to it? It can be an absolutely amazing dream, but somehow it just slips away as you leave your sleep and face the reality of your day. Sometimes all you have left is the memory that you had a good dream in the first place, but no recall of the dream itself.

I love my country, but I have this fear: For too many, the American Dream might feel just like that.

Someone once told me that writing a book is either "inside you" or not. If it is, it's just a matter of letting it out. That's been me for ten years now. Finally, in early 2017, on the first day I seriously thought about actually doing this, I wrote down six themes:

Create Amazing
WHY?
WHAT?

WHO?

HOW?

Only in America

I immediately knew that the most important question was *Why*? And I began to write this book:

Because the right answer to *why* should be the cornerstone piece to one of America's greatest challenges: economic injustice.

Because the gap between the haves and the have-nots is not only widening unconscionably, it's also in direct opposition to the aspiration of our country.

Because we can do better than this.

I wrote this book because the founders of this nation said so . . . because they had the right *Why*.

Exactly What Is *Why*?

Helen is *Why*. Every day, the American Dream is awakened by Helen. She heads to work before the sun comes up, carpooling with Dan and LaShonda because she can't afford to fix her car. The American Dream is steaming from the coffee-to-go cup that Manuel grabs at his favorite café so he can make his 8 AM meeting with an important new client. After months without a job, the American Dream is wearing out the soles of Tim's shoes. The American Dream is standing room only at Jill's new restaurant, but never quite big enough for Dave to buy a home.

Yet for Merrie, the American Dream came true, and it still does every time she watches the sunset over her retirement dream home at the Lake of the Ozarks, Missouri.

Helen, Dan, LaShonda, Manuel, Tim, Jill, Dave, and Merrie are all *Why* someone needed to write this book. I'm proud it was me.

Even I was *Why*.

I hope by the end of this book, you'll have your *Why,* too.

Everyone working for a living or looking for work is about the business of the American Dream, even if the American Dream isn't always open for business.

It can be. It should be.

This book is about what it takes to open that dream, who you'll need, and how to do it. But critically, it's about *why* employee ownership works, and just as important, why this proven business model can create a more solvent, sane, and equitable economy for millions more

> When the employees are the owners and the owners are the employees, the outcomes can be exponentially higher . . . for the firm . . . for its people . . . for our country.

Americans. Even more specifically, this book is about Employee Stock Ownership Plans, or *ESOP*s, and why employee ownership is a sustainable solution to the mounting economic injustice that compromises the principles of our nation.

The ESOP is not a theory. It is a proven approach that can lead to better profitability and a greater purpose—*if done right.*

Why? Because owners work harder; because owners care more. When the employees are the owners and the owners are the employees, the outcomes can be exponentially higher . . . for the firm . . . for its people . . . for our country. Taken to its fullest, every employee owning every share can make the place hum. And that hum, I promise you, is the sound of the American Dream coming true.

Putting That in Writing

The day after jotting down my first notes for this book, I started reading. I'll admit, I didn't realize how much I'd have to *read* in order to *write*. I wanted to see if my book of lived experience was already written and available in stores. It wasn't, but my message about American employee ownership has indeed been addressed by some gifted academicians with deep roots in the American marketplace.

The Citizen's Share by Joseph Blasi and Douglas Kruse of Rutgers University and Harvard's Richard Freeman is seminal. It's a brilliant, highly recommended tome on economic inequality in America that, among other themes, argues through research how employee ownership can provide an important solution to solving the complicated puzzle of American enterprise.

To my joy and true to my own experience, Blasi, Kruse, and Freeman affirmed what I believe about the American Dream and how we can (and should) help millions more Americans reach it. Our forefathers intended America to be different from other nations in that it would be founded on the principles of individual liberty, private property rights, and equal justice for all. This theory of "American exceptionalism" directly correlates with the intent of employee ownership. From theory to practice, the amazing outcome potential of employee ownership is entirely grounded by research. Blasi, Kruse, and Freeman confirmed that employees who own the stock of the firms where they work are more likely to stay, show greater pride in their work, work harder, and make more suggestions as to how to improve the place. Further, in the end, they're happier and better paid.[1]

Sound good to you?

A Stronger Platform

For the nation's next presidential election, there will be no better time for every wannabe-in-chief to strengthen their platform with a solid ESOP plank. While candidates promote a variety of fixatives, they often "overlook, however, the principle set of relations that skew American capitalism upward: the ownership and operational control of business enterprises," according to John Case in his article "An Economy in Waiting."[2]

Here's Hoping Future Presidential Hopefuls Find This Book

With the 2018 passage of the Main Street Employee Ownership Act, Congress created a clearer path for the ESOP solution. Just in time, according to Blasi, for "the hundreds of thousands of small businesses owned by retiring baby boomers that are at risk of closing up, putting millions of jobs on the line as well."[3]

As an argument for economic justice that could strengthen either Democratic or Republican platforms, Case imagines "our candidate storms to the forefront of the primary scrum by making employee ownership a central issue in his or her campaign." If only. Case's "Economy in Waiting" acknowledges that ESOP doesn't easily lend itself to a bumper sticker, but neither does the "top-heavy and civically unsustainable ownership structure of the existing investment economy—noting, for example, the fact that the top tenth of Americans control 84 percent of all American-owned stock."[4]

Here's more great news for all candidates: Employee ownership is overwhelmingly supported by conservatives and liberals alike.[5]

COMPANY CHOICE BY IDEOLOGICAL VIEWS

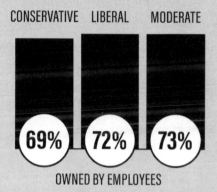

CONSERVATIVE   LIBERAL   MODERATE

69%   72%   73%

OWNED BY EMPLOYEES

"Understanding Support for ESOPs" | Dr. Joseph Blasi

According to 2014 U.S. Department of Labor data on ESOPs, Blasi and company found that "about two million workers and managers were invested in about 5,800 closely held companies with the total employee ownership valued at $255 billion. While the average ESOP worker in these companies has an ownership stake of $134,000, our calculations are this is close to a quarter of a million dollars for workers who stay with the company for 20 years."[6]

Isn't it time for ESOPs to be ticker-tape paraded down Wall Street and every Main Street to celebrate the economic justice they've already delivered to Americans working at the almost 7,000 employee-owned companies today? "Successful ones—as most are—enable employees to build up serious wealth over time," wrote Case, citing the Rutgers study. "Some have a million or more."[7]

To anyone running for office: Isn't it time for this nation to wake up to this very real version of the American Dream?

Owners Work Harder. Owners Care More.

How's this for *Why*: 100 percent of your employee owners can reap 100 percent of the reward for the difference they make—and that difference, I promise you, is going to be huge.

The empirical evidence cited by Blasi and others in the field confirmed my experience from the ground level—one employee owner at a time. I will further argue that what's happening in private companies across the country would likely blow away the results of employee-ownership benefit programs at the biggest public companies. *In fact, I'm certain of it.* Taken to its fullest, every employee owning every share—100 percent employee ownership—can produce a quantum leap forward for companies in almost any and every sector.

The good news is Dr. Blasi and team are already working on gathering that exact data.

What It's Not

Before we go too far, I've got to stress this important point: Employee ownership is not, will never be, and would never work as an idea for the redistribution of wealth in America. Economic inequality in America is a problem—a big one—but socialism or ideas similar to it are no solution, in my view.

Employee ownership is not socialism-meets-capitalism. Indeed, employee ownership without the right management or the right performance incentives—without the right "it"—is just another benefit program. No, thank you.

What It Is

Employee ownership is capitalism on steroids. And if done right, employee ownership, by its very definition, will result in a predominantly fairer distribution of successful capitalism. Indeed, the citizens can get their share.[8]

Employee ownership is a path to building wealth with better distribution. Moreover, it is a path toward building more wealth, perhaps much more wealth, yet still with substantially fairer distribution than exists in the America we know today.

Getting to Great

My favorite all-time read and business guru is Jim Collins. In a single one-hour phone call about whether this book needed writing, he made a substantial impact on my message, which will become very clear. Yes, I have a serious man-crush on this guy. His best seller, *Good to Great,* was my work-bible and personal inspiration when I was the CEO and chairman of the international engineering and construction powerhouse Burns & McDonnell, a firm I believe stands as an employee-owned beacon to industry today.

> Employee ownership is capitalism on steroids. And if done right, employee ownership, by its very definition, will result in a predominantly fairer distribution of successful capitalism. Indeed, the citizens can get their share.

During my final year at Burns & Mac, at our annual management retreat, my chief administrative officer, Melissa Wood, and company president Ray Kowalik (who would succeed me as CEO) surprised me with a special appearance by Jim Collins. I was so hero-struck, I don't recall much of the day. But on the front of a picture of the two of us taken before his talk, he wrote, "*You're Level 5.*" Other than "Gramps," I can't imagine a better title.

Collins proclaims that "good is the enemy of great." My company was *good*. But in 1986, 100 percent employee ownership gave us the opportunity to become *great*. It wasn't due to the Burns or the McDonnell families, or any of our five other CEOs over the span of 122 years. It was the employee owners of our firm that made us great. And each was finally rewarded fully for their contribution.

Sounds trite, but it is exactly true.

Greg Graves and Jim Collins (2016)

In the next chapter about the Burns & McDonnell ESOP story, I'll share the firm's path from partnership; to acquisition candidate; to public corporation division; to near dissolution; and, finally, to explosive growth as a 100 percent employee-owned firm. You'll see the employment and revenue numbers grow, languish, and ultimately explode—all organically.

So, read on. *Create Amazing* will show you what a growing body of research indicates about the potential for employee ownership, especially in America. Better still, it'll take you under the surface into the solid, evidence-based reasons for establishing an ESOP and explain *What*, *Who*, *How*, and, most importantly, *Why* you should.

CHAPTER 1

Create Amazing

The Burns & Mac Story: A Successful ESOP in Action

This book is not meant to be a Burns & McDonnell biography—not even remotely. Those should never be written by former CEOs like me. But if you're going to have any basis for my perspective on *Why, What, Who,* and *How,* I have to give you my own favorite version of 100 percent employee ownership—our company.

Throughout the chapters that follow, I'll share other examples as well to illustrate that the ESOP journey to greatness has been accomplished by many companies, usually with outstanding results. But let there be no doubt—it isn't always a nice, smooth ascent. I won't ever promise this will be easy. In fact, I can almost guarantee that it won't be—but I can promise you this: It will be worth it.

Creating Amazing

In August 2014, I joined my chief administrative officer, Melissa "Mel" Wood, and Director of Corporate Marketing Melissa Lavin (a.k.a. the "Melissas") in the Burns & Mac boardroom, where the co-CEOs of Signal Theory were waiting. The CEOs were Ali Mahaffy and John January, a couple of Kansas City up-and-coming entrepreneurs I would soon recognize as pure geniuses in their field of brand development, marketing, and design. But in that moment, I was tentative at best. As CEO of a successful, 100-plus-year-old company, I was not anxious to fix what clearly wasn't broken.

Lavin and Wood, along with Mahaffy and January, were about to present their ideas for a new company logo, a branding campaign, and a new catchphrase that they promised would encompass everything I believed about our employee-owned firm.

Full disclosure: I was hoping they'd bomb. It took everything I had not to roll my eyes as I took my seat.

Melissa Lavin began. She presented all the different logos Burns & Mac had used over the last 116 years. I held our current logo borderline vigilantly but, to be honest, I was swayed by the retrospective on different versions we'd had over the many decades. Seeing all the versions showed me how we'd grown and reminded me of my own gospel that change is healthy.

Now it was Signal Theory's turn. Ali Mahaffy started with a presentation of all the interviews they had done across the company asking employee owners how they felt about our firm and its brand. They got the answers I expected. Our people didn't just love the place—*they loved it like they owned it.* As she talked, the logo on the big screen slowly started to morph. These consultants—they're tricky ones, that's for sure. Just when I was prepared not to like what they were bringing, the ampersand in Burns & McDonnell evolved into something new . . . something that felt like us *now*—strong and solid and melded—both consistent with yet different from us back then.

And damn . . . I *loved* it.

At least until John January began to give some sort of sermon. Instantly, I was late for the door—this kind of thing is not my scene. Let the record show, I loved and respected both Melissas, so even though my urge to run was almost unrestrainable, I made myself listen to what John was saying.

John's Pitch

For more than one hundred years, people have associated words such as engineering, architecture, construction, and consulting with our company. And while these words may describe some of the things we do, they don't scratch the surface of what Burns & McDonnell is really all about. Because, if you think about it, you'll realize that together, we make some pretty amazing things possible.

You see, this isn't about building a new smart substation. This is about creating a sustainable solution that can serve as a model for the world. This isn't about a new design for a structure. It's about creating a space that will improve the lives of those who occupy it. And this isn't about winning a new project. This is about helping a client uncover a solution they never dreamed was possible.

What we do isn't about what we design and build. What we do is about making the world a more amazing place.

And while most people take for granted the millions of details that go into making amazing happen, all of us at Burns & McDonnell know that it does not happen by chance. Behind every amazing act, there is an amazing person poring over every nook and cranny of the plans one more time. Catching a red-eye flight to work through a challenge face-to-face . . . taking a calculated risk on a young talent. Because, in the end, amazing is a mindset. The kind of mindset shared by people with an entrepreneurial stake in the future of our company and the world.

And while, on the surface, some of the things we do may not seem glamorous or even all that easy for our families to understand when we talk about them at the dinner table, in the end, we are responsible for some pretty amazing things.

We tame rivers and capture the wind.

We optimize energy and bolster economies.

We build communities and improve lives.

We inspire minds and provide work with lasting impact.

We're about amazing our clients, our competition, and, occasionally, even ourselves by taking on the industry's biggest challenges with some of the world's best thinking. We're about creating amazing opportunities for great people. And we're about making our world a more amazing place, one project at a time. This is why we've been in business since 1898. This is why we have created lasting partnerships that are more personal than business. And it's why you've chosen to be here today.

Burns & McDonnell. Create Amazing.

They had done it. Everything this firm meant to me—thirty-four years of employment, twenty-eight as an owner, ten as CEO, and six as chairman—came out in just two words: *Create Amazing.* That was exactly how I felt about this place, and *create amazing* was precisely what we did as a company. And we would go on to prove it.

- We'd be named one of *Fortune* magazine's Top 100 Places to Work ten times (and counting).
- We'd be named the *Best Large Firm* service provider in our industry by PSMJ Resources.
- We'd grow the firm 400 percent in employee owners and 1,000 percent in revenue; and, best of all, we'd grow the firm's foundation 1,000 percent in just thirteen years.

From that meeting forward, as CEO, I spoke those two words, "*create amazing*," over and over again in every presentation, at every meeting, to the widest audience possible—always adding, "for our clients, for our communities, for each other."

> From that meeting forward, as CEO, I spoke those two words, "*create amazing*," over and over again in every presentation, at every meeting, to the widest audience possible—always adding, "for our clients, for our communities, for each other."

To be honest, I don't know if the founders of this organization had a goal that lofty, but the Melissas and I certainly did.

Unlikely Partners

Robert E. McDonnell and Clinton S. Burns were not your typical college pals destined to be entrepreneurial partners. They were from different geographical areas of the country and from wildly different economic backgrounds. For reasons both economic and academic, it took McDonnell six years to go from high school to college graduate, while Burns, according to every historical note, was the smartest person in every room. Somehow, the two forged a friendship and decided to

Future American president Herbert Hoover on R. E. McDonnell's survey crew at Stanford. Signed later by President Hoover while in the White House.

become partners. But, after graduating from Stanford in May 1897, they couldn't even agree on where their new firm should reside. Burns went East. McDonnell stayed West.

Fortunately for us, they maintained a correspondence. In early 1898, they agreed to meet in Salt Lake City, Utah, to work on what would become the most important business plan in the history of the company. Seeking the most potential clients within one day's travel of a major city, they targeted towns that still didn't have access to clean drinking water, reliable wastewater facilities, and affordable electricity for streetlights. After a month of studying, they chose Kansas City as the ideal base of operation. On April 1, 1898, the engineering firm of Burns & McDonnell was born.

Just two guys, Burns & McDonnell. They were both the owners and the only employees. While ESOPs didn't exist yet, employee ownership was already fueling the esprit de corps that would phenomenally provide a return on their investment.

Robert E. McDonnell and Clinton S. Burns (1898)

From Father to Son

I cannot imagine many tougher management challenges than the transition of leadership from father to son.

Family-owned businesses in America that successfully make it beyond the first generation are not common—Walmart being the most well-known example. Kansas City has beat the odds with a number of companies not only staying in the family through the second generation, but actually becoming substantially more successful. Companies like Hallmark, JE Dunn Construction, and our two biggest banks (UMB and Commerce) come immediately to mind.

For Burns & Mac, it also played out this way: In 1924, Clinton Burns died of throat cancer at fifty-two years old, exactly twenty-six years after starting the company. His daughter, Miriam, was never involved in the firm. R. E. "Mr. Mac" McDonnell worked for the firm as its owner and managing partner for fifty-three years before semi-retiring in 1951 and transitioning it to his son, R. H. "Bob" McDonnell.

Bob was not his dad. Dad was a nationally recognized leader in his field, having been published 160 times, whereas Son was Kansas City's preeminent people person—Bob was everyone's friend.

According to many, Bob McDonnell was the best salesman in town, and the firm expanded robustly under his leadership. Bob quickly became one of the most successful businessmen in Kansas City and he wasn't afraid to show it. Known for his fur coats and fancy cars, Bob was also famous for successfully recruiting and managing the firm's engineering talent. His legendary desk remains at the firm complete with a secret compartment where he hid the liquor always on hand to celebrate the firm's wins.

End of an Era

Bob McDonnell rapidly expanded the firm, including its areas of service. He helped the firm land its first projects in aviation, industrial, and environmental engineering.

But if father-to-son is a tough transition, son-to–third generation in American enterprise is usually next to impossible. Again, I can name a

R. E. McDonnell, center front; son R. H. McDonnell, center back (1929)

couple of exceptions (a friend of mine who appreciates his privacy is the best I've ever known), but successful American third-generation family-owned companies are the extreme exception. Perhaps if more family-owned businesses were transitioned to daughters, history would be different.

Like most, Burns & McDonnell did not make it to generation three. Instead, Bob McDonnell elected to put the firm up for sale in 1971 as he approached his own retirement. While sad, it was eventually the best outcome possible. Bob had brought a few people from his leadership team into a corporate partnership; they were big winners. The vast majority were losers (a few of whom I got to know personally, including one future CEO).

Owners won. Employees lost. Typical story.

The successful bidder and new owner was Armco Steel. Their emerging corporate strategy was to divest away from their core business and they were doing numerous acquisitions away from steel manufacturing, including insurance and professional services. Burns & McDonnell became the flagship of their Professional Services Division.

The Perfect Gentleman

Speaking of tough transitions, if there's a more complicated changeover of executive leadership than father-to-son and on to a third generation, it might just be what Ray Luhnow, who was only the third CEO in seventy-three years, faced.

Luhnow was up against Bob McDonnell himself, who still came in to work (often in his new Rolls-Royce), along with a retiring group of former partners who had just cashed out. Then there was Armco itself—the out-of-town boss from a megacorporation (500 times the size of Burns & Mac) that was looking for an immediate return on its investment. Combine all that with a company full of employees who no longer knew what long-term careers at Burns & Mac might look like. *Complicated* might not be strong enough to describe the dynamics.

Fortunately, Ray Luhnow was the man for the job—the definition of a perfect gentleman. Despite the obstacles, he had one great thing going for

(left to right) Ray Luhnow with future CEOs Newt Campbell,
Dave Ruf, and Greg Graves (2004)

him: The American coal-fired electric business was booming, and thanks
to it, Burns & Mac was growing . . . growing fast.

The Father of the Burns & Mac ESOP

Newt Campbell was leading the company's booming Power Division as
Ray Luhnow's retirement approached. Despite the company's Armageddon of 1981–82, when massive layoffs occurred, Newt was the easy choice
to become the firm's fourth CEO in 1982. He didn't stay long though,
having been promoted by Armco to lead their overall Professional Services
Division in 1984.

For those of us still in the trenches and who survived the firm's con-
traction (from almost 1,400 employees to roughly 600), prospects would
soon look better. A lot of environmental regulations were passed or significantly amended in the late 1970s and early 1980s, including the Clean Air
Act. Soon the company was, at least, no longer shrinking rapidly.

You couldn't say that for the American steel industry. It was in a full free
fall. In the ten years from 1976 to 1986, more than 300,000 steel workers

permanently lost their jobs due to a slumping economy and often subsidized foreign competition. As a result, Armco was approaching possible complete default. Armco decided in early 1985 to intentionally implode to its core. Newt was given the task of selling off the Professional Services Division, including its flagship, Burns & McDonnell Engineering Company.

So the father of our ESOP, Newt Campbell, went to work. His task was made even tougher by the fact that not a single former partner from the time of the sale to Armco was still at the firm. At the majority of successful private company–to-ESOP transitions, there are a core of executives who understand the special rewards and duties of ownership, according to research from Rutgers.[1] Burns & Mac had none.

Let's take a close look at the company in 1985 to better unpack the transition.

May 1985: Armco officially announces it will be selling its Professional Services Division—including Burns & McDonnell.

June 1985: Newt Campbell and others meet with Philadelphia-based management consultants from The Coxe Group. They recommend the idea of forming Burns & Mac as an ESOP.

July 1985: Newt Campbell and company president Dave Ruf begin regular, all-employee meetings announcing the idea and their support for a 100 percent ESOP buyout.

July 1985: The firm brings in ESOP-ERISA, legal, tax, banking, and acquisition consultants.

August 1985: After nail-biting negotiations, Armco elects to decline a higher bid from German diesel manufacturer Klöckner-Humboldt-Deutz and allows the employees of Burns & McDonnell to buy the firm. Details of the negotiations continue through December. The firm agrees to a five-year payout of a percent of its profits back to Armco to sweeten the deal.

The purchase price is confidential, but taking all factors into account, it's about 30 percent of what the firm was purchased for originally by Armco.

Nearly eighty years after local Kansas City banker William Kemper advised Burns & McDonnell on the profitable sale of an Ozark property in 1907, another Kemper played a pivotal role in the history and success of the firm. Grandson R. Crosby Kemper Jr. was now CEO and chairman of UMB (United Missouri Bank)—the only bank in America that agreed to make the loan to Burns & McDonnell for a 100 percent employee buyout in 1985. UMB did require that the firm's ten officers personally finance a portion of the loan balance—approximately 17 percent of the company. Somehow, they did.

One of those officers was Joel Cerwick, who would eventually become my early board chair. "I was the youngest guy in the group with the least amount of money (and I had to borrow mine) when we bought the company," Cerwick recalled. "Then we turned it over to the employees—giving them an opportunity to buy stock. This meant everybody had some skin in the game—because what's good for the company ended up being good for every employee in it. We had maybe six hundred employees at the time and when the ten of us became the management, several quit. They didn't have any faith in us. Honestly, we didn't know a lot about what we were doing yet. But those who left back then are probably sorry they did!"[2]

By the end of 1986, bookings were strong and Burns & McDonnell was well on its way to becoming a thriving ESOP.

"We couldn't believe the profit we made," said Darrell Hosler, former executive vice president. "Even at the end of the first year, we could distribute bonuses and put more money in the ESOP account for the benefit of the employees when they vested. The growth was due to the fact that we, the employees, owned it ourselves. Owners work harder because they'll benefit directly. They're earning incentive pay."[3]

The Big Ten

Back in 1985 when Newt Campbell let his nine other officers know that they'd each have to invest their own funds to keep the doors open at Burns & Mac, the news wasn't received enthusiastically. The firm was still struggling from the early 1980s, and it would be a hardship for most of them to personally raise that kind of cash. But each one did. Some didn't stay long enough to reap the rewards, but without all of them, what happened next would not have been possible.

Hats off to the guys I call *The Big Ten*:

Newt Campbell
Dave Ruf
Darrell Hosler
Joel Cerwick
John Riley
John Williams
Doug Criner
Jim Tearney
Bill Nofsinger
John Hoffman

Yes, they were all white guys—such was the demographic of the engineering profession of that time—but none were wealthy or privileged, just committed. Burns & McDonnell should regard them all with the highest respect possible for as long as this great run continues.

The Bulldog

I'm not 100 percent certain, but I'm pretty sure that Burns & Mac's fifth CEO, Dave G. Ruf Jr. himself, would agree with this: If Newt Campbell was our ESOP's father, Dave was, without question, its bulldog. He was— easily—the toughest boss any of us ever had. Dave also had the distinction of becoming the firm's CEO twice—once when Newt was promoted to Armco, and the second time when Newt retired from Burns & McDonnell in 1994.

Now Dave was firmly in charge, with an emphasis on *firmly* and *in charge.* His leadership style was as different from Newt's as you could possibly imagine. Come to think of it, it was also as different from mine as it

Newt Campbell and Dave Ruf burn the mortgage with R. Crosby Kemper Jr. (1994).

could possibly be. I remember another former boss of mine and senior officer jokingly accusing Dave of always ruling with the stick. Dave didn't like that much and countered that he motivated with the carrot just as often for those who were successful (which was absolutely true). My buddy who ran one of the firm's most successful divisions lamented, "I know you use the carrot, boss, but you're always hitting me with it."

Dave had one of the keenest eyes for talent I have ever witnessed. On his watch, some of our most important officers and future board members were recruited, and he deserves almost sole credit for championing our move to our firm's first-class world headquarters.

I have to say there was one person in my career who strongly influenced me, and he was Dave Ruf. He drilled into us the importance of hard work. Even before we were an ESOP, our CEO Dave Ruf would put in "Ruf time" (7:30 AM to 5:30 PM versus 8 AM to 5 PM), which enforced an attitude that you'd put in extra time without being paid. When Graves became CEO, we asked him about Ruf time and he said, "Well, that's a good start." In other words, everyone should want to work extra for the company, maybe even more. There has always been an expectation for hard work, and working extra.

You've got to be an employee who can do that. An ESOP is not a place for the guy who wants to spend a lot of time hanging around the water cooler.

—*Carl Weilert, principal and former employee owner, Burns & McDonnell*

There's a lesson here: Employee ownership success doesn't require one specific style of leadership. Under Newt's academic style, the firm's success got a foothold. Under Dave's authoritarian rule, it took off. Would that style work today? No, I don't think so, but it certainly did then.

> For me, there was a new and bigger question: Employee ownership was always great for Burns & McDonnell and its clients, *but* was Burns & McDonnell always great for the employee owners— the people who were making us successful in the first place?

You'll Be Great

I have always assumed the positive. I was clearly the cheerleader-type CEO and simply loved reminding my team, "You'll be great."

When I became president of the firm in the summer of 2002, Burns & Mac was already a good place to work and a great place to retire from, but there was more to accomplish . . . a lot more. In the eighteen months I waited to become the firm's sixth CEO, I had the chance of a lifetime to simply study the firm I loved. I saw the potential greatness of what we were doing in the look on every employee-owner's face. I felt the synergy of working together as owners, and I realized that we were already *truly great* at the "work" because we were all invested in the same success—every oar was pulling hard in the same direction.

For me, there was a new and bigger question: Employee ownership was always great for Burns & McDonnell and its clients, *but* was Burns & McDonnell always great for the employee owners—the people who were making us successful in the first place?

Greg with mega-client Steve Swinson (TECO) and Construction
Group president Don Greenwood (2011)

If I'm proud of anything, I'm proud that we focused on that.

In 2009, we got a big thumbs-up from *Fortune* magazine when we were named the 50th best place to work in America (we would eventually rise all the way to number fourteen). Melissa Wood was vice president of Human Resources in 2009, and she brought me the exciting news. We were ecstatic. After some celebrating, I tasked Mel with this job: Go find out who ranked number one and why. I may or may not have added ". . . our employee-ownership culture will kick their butt."

A few days later, Melissa reported back. *Fortune* ranked Google the number-one place to work in America. It turns out Google had a free

Burns & Mac makes *Fortune*'s list for the first time (2009)

Officers and about 2,500 Kansas City–based employee owners (2014)

health clinic, no designated work hours, and no dress code. They offered free or discounted childcare and sported Olympic-quality workout facilities on-site. They also provided their employees with free or discounted breakfast, lunch, and dinner. Oh yeah—they also had pet care.

"Okay, Mel," I said, "how about you go find out who number two is. We'll kick their butt instead."

And Today: A Project Manager Takes Charge

The company's seventh CEO (in 122 years) is Ray Kowalik. Ray is probably the most talented of any of us, and certainly the tallest. He was perhaps the best project manager I ever had the joy of promoting. The company has continued and will continue to soar under his leadership.

He's already moved the firm into direct hire construction, expanded the world headquarters, and broken pretty much every sales and share price record.

Good friends Ray Kowalik and Greg (2016)

Burns & Mac Is *Why*

My all-time best, greatest place to work is Burns & Mac, even without pet care, and even if the Eagles perform live in some other firm's parking lot every Friday afternoon. I absolutely know this without having worked at any of those kinds of places. I know this because employee ownership makes work more than a job—it makes it personal. The truth is that I loved my time serving alongside the employee owners of Burns & McDonnell for thirty-eight years so much, I simply cannot put my feelings into words. I guess you might call it equal parts duty and pure love. Thanks to the employee owners of our firm and their incredible work, I was able to retire at fifty-nine to chase a few more of life's ambitions, including chairing the boards of a world-class hospital and our local repertory theater. I've built a dream house on our own Lake Deanna, and I'm finishing this book.

Burns & McDonnell owes me nothing. It gave me the American Dream . . . I am forever in its debt.

And, for a kid who peddled newspapers from his bike in the bitter cold of a South Dakota youth, that's my personal *Why.*

Yes, I know a lot of *What* there is to know about ESOPs, but experts with the right letters behind their names will be cited often in this book. And I have very strong opinions as to *Who* you want on your team and *How* an employee-owned company should be run, based on experience and broad evidence. But the biggest question you should ask first—the one with the most important answer—is *Why?*

CHAPTER 2

WHY?

The Most Important Question Is the Most Important Place to Start

Economic justice doesn't have to be about giving money away. Wealth should be earned—and it can be—equitably.

Why should you start an Employee Stock Ownership Plan or convert your company to an ESOP? Or maybe make the big leap to a 100 percent employee-owned company?

The short answer: It's not only better for the people (your employees) who have made you successful, but it's for a better America as well. Those are two pretty good places to start, don't you think?

> Wealth should be earned—and it can be—equitably.

Take It Back If You Must

If you bought this book because you've heard or read that ESOPs are a great way to avoid taxes and you're searching hard to put one over on the IRS, well, you're partly right—but your *Why* is wrong. You're asking the wrong question, and this is not your book. You have my permission to return it and ask for your money back.

If you bought this book because you don't believe your employees work hard enough or appreciate your brilliance deeply enough, not to mention all the risks you've taken, and are now hoping that adding a small percentage ESOP into the mix will do the trick, well, you might actually be right. But your *Why* is way off. Return this book. I really don't want you to read it.

Maybe you bought this book because you love your employees and you want the best for them. Maybe you want them to own a piece of the pie. So, you're going to add a fairly large new employee company-stock benefit program. Well, close, but I am asking you now and in the pages that follow to reconsider your *Why into something much bigger.*

In this chapter, I'm going to convince you why you should go all in with an ESOP. At that point, if you can't make the big leap—the 100 percent leap for all the right reasons—then, as much as this kills me, return the book and get your money back.

If you want your company to perform at its absolute peak, and you want the people who make that happen (you included) to receive the ultimate financial return—that of an owner—then *read on*. This is going to be fun.

Don't panic . . . you're not going to read anything here about giving the place away. But I am asking you to set it free . . . free to reach places you didn't know your business could go . . . free to create an amazing company and leave a much bigger legacy both in your business and your country.

Here's *Why*.

Why? Because Thomas Jefferson Was Right

Think about why our nation has been successful. When Thomas Jefferson agonized over the details of the Louisiana Purchase, he wasn't thinking that it would make *him* rich, he was thinking that it would make *America* rich. More importantly, Jefferson believed it would make individual

Americans prosper. Jefferson knew from the earliest days of the American experience—even before the Revolution—that individual landowners (the original American entrepreneurs) would out-work, out-think, out-sweat, *and* out-perform their European counterparts if—and only if—they owned the property themselves. It was a principle worth fighting for in a land that had just wrenched its freedom from monarchy.

"The Earth is given as a common stock for man to labor and live on. The small landowners are the most precious part of a state," as Jefferson saw it.[1] America may not have been born the day he paid France $15,000,000 in 1803 for "Louisiana," but the biggest and best example of the American economic advantage was.

Just one year later, in 1804, the Lewis and Clark Expedition was moving up the Missouri River, and America was headed west.

Future presidents Madison, Polk, Johnson, and others furthered Jefferson's expansion and economic path through treaty, acquisition, and outright cession. President Abraham Lincoln's Homestead Act of 1862 made 10 percent of the land of our entire nation available to small farmers.

None of these ventures were without cost or risk, both in dollars and in lives. They were not always America's proudest moments. But they were all based on a belief in the entrepreneurship of the American people and were driven by the concept of autonomous ownership.

The proof is clear. In 1776, the American economy was barely 30 percent the size of Britain's economy. Less than one hundred years later, in 1871, the United States became the world's largest economy, and remains so still today, with an estimated gross domestic product of more than $22 trillion in 2020. Jefferson was right. Ownership works.

> Jefferson knew from the earliest days of the American experience that individual landowners would out-work, out-think, out-sweat, *and* out-perform their European counterparts if—and only if—they owned the property themselves.

Why? Because the American Dream
Requires Productivity

The Citizen's Share: Putting Ownership Back into Democracy describes five unique studies aimed at the subject of productivity in firms offering at least some portion of profit sharing and/or ownership to their employees. The studies were done by the Treasury of the United Kingdom (2007), the *Journal for Applied Psychology* (2006), the University of California, Berkeley (2003), Joseph Blasi and his team at Rutgers (2000), and the General Accounting Office of the U.S. Congress (1987). The results were validated in all five studies: Employees who share in the capital experience of the firm where they work are more productive—often much more productive.[2]

Productivity is the key measure in these *Why* examples. American or European public corporations weren't going to simply reward their employees with ownership out of the goodness of their hearts if they didn't believe the productivity gains from such a move would be of eventual benefit to their outside shareholders. The results validated what numerous ESOPs in America were already showing: Faith in the worker, combined with tangible reward, would duplicate Jefferson's landowner success.

This compilation of work led to arguably the most important modern vetting of the Jeffersonian playbook, *The Shared Capitalism Research Project*. Undertaken in 2000 by the National Bureau of Economic Research (NBER) in Cambridge under the direction of Blasi and team, the NBER study focused on the worker, not just the firm. More than 40,000 workers took part. The results spoke loudly when the study was published in 2009.[3]

The idea of directly focusing research on workers and their motives was a significant change to the data collection but was a brilliant new hypothesis as to the cause and effect of productivity improvement. It says, as ESOPs well know, that it is not simply the benefit but the perception of the worker to capital participation that is the most important driver to actual change in behavior. Remember—*this is really important*—these results are based on employees having *only a share* of interest in the companies where they work—sometimes far short of the 100 percent interest that's possible.

The research showed that employees with even a relatively small capital interest in their firms' success . . .

- were more likely to stay
- had greater loyalty and pride
- expressed greater willingness to work hard
- made more suggestions for improvement

And, in the end, those employees believed that they had better wages and working conditions, thanks to their ownership stake.

What Blasi and team demonstrated clearly is that productivity gains through loyalty, hard work, and true participative behavior are not just possible *but* predictable when employees become owners through capital sharing.

> Selling the benefit is not just part of the story; it is critical to it.

Even more important, it demonstrates that the worker perception of ownership might be even more causational than the benefit itself. Selling the benefit is not just part of the story; it is critical to it.

The Owner Advantage

Have you ever noticed the difference in restaurant service when the waiters are working primarily for tips versus servers in dining establishments where everyone is paid the same no matter what? Functionally, that waiter is owning it. They are their own business with a ton of skin in the game. It all comes down to ownership—both in terms of motivation and accountability. Owners work harder than non-owners.

I've been both . . . give me the owner every time.

Excuse a moment of negativity, but so often in America we get this wrong. My dad was union-strong, and people who know me well will tell you I've always supported union causes within Burns & Mac's construction group. But I have equally and always rejected an all-too-common union leadership stance that management is somehow the enemy—that employees need work only as hard and as long each day as it takes to avoid being fired. Of course, I also abhor the equally ridiculous notion held by too many American firms and their leaders that employees should be paid just barely enough to keep them from quitting. *Both schools of thought churn out owner-versus-employee mediocrity, if not actual animosity.* They result in low productivity, poor morale, and a climate of divisiveness that pits workers against employers.

> Open your eyes. There's so much more. There isn't just a middle ground here; there is a productivity nirvana to be found. When everyone's an owner, everyone's got skin in the game. And that can lead to one of the best economic win-win scenarios possible.

It's a totally different culture. Because everyone is an owner, Burns & McDonnell really is your company and people tend to take better care of what they own. We really try to make the best business decisions. We'll take an early morning or really late flight to save money for the company . . . the list goes on.

—Michelle Word, Burns & McDonnell Diversity Advocate

Open your eyes. There's so much more. There isn't just a middle ground here; there is a productivity nirvana to be found. When everyone's an owner, everyone's got skin in the game. And that can lead to one of the best economic win-win scenarios possible.

The rise of unions in America was the direct result of worker abuse. Collective bargaining, thank goodness, fixed much of this. Today, a mountain of research shows that owner, worker, and country can all benefit from a new approach where each is dependent on the success of all.

Why? Because Jim Collins Says So

The first time I met Jim Collins, the aforementioned best-selling author and business guru, was at a conference for CEOs of the top fifty construction companies in America in 2010. Collins was the headliner of the event. Sometimes I wonder if he understood the impact he would have on us—he certainly changed my executive life that day. He forever reshaped my *Why*.

Collins asked for a show of hands. "How many people here have only one direct report?" Only one hand went up. He walked to about the middle of the room and asked, "Do they really even pay you?" Everyone chuckled. I knew that guy and I never liked him . . . I was loving this . . . so far.

Then he asked if anyone had more than ten direct reports. Again, only one hand, but this time it was mine.

Actually, at that time, I had fifteen direct reports. Collins came all the way to the back of the room, looked me right in the eye, and asked, "Happily married?" Yes, I said, but he just laughed along with everyone else and walked away. For a moment, hero worship was dead.

Finally, Collins asked, "How many people here have six to seven direct reports?" Almost every remaining hand went up. Then he posed this simple and brilliant question: "If six to seven individuals dictate nearly all of your success, why would you tolerate any one of them being anything short of spectacular?" You could have heard a pin drop as he let the room ponder. This is how he introduced one of the most important tenets of his most famous book, *Good to Great*: You have to start with "who" before you get to "what." *Who* is about taking your business journey with the right people—and getting those people in the right seats on your bus. Just as important, before you can do that, you have to get the wrong people the hell off your bus. I took notes feverishly, and when I looked around, every CEO in the room was doing the same.

Collins's "Hedgehog Concept" and the "Stockdale Paradox" grounded me in understanding the common denominators of successful businesses. But his bus analogy, along with his "Flywheel" and "Level 5 Leadership" principles are my favorites in terms of their direct application to employee-ownership success.

With due credit and profound gratitude to Jim for allowing me to paraphrase his work and wisdom, I'll make three points in relation to *Why* employee ownership works:

1. These are owners (not just "employees") on your bus.

If there were only two owners in your business and you were one of them, how would it feel if the other was working less, working on the wrong things, or maybe even having lower standards than you? You get the idea. Would that change if you were one of five owners? Ten? A thousand?

Increasing the number of owners doesn't change anything. In fact, it only makes it more obvious if you don't have the right people. In a 100 percent employee-ownership culture, everyone is looking to make everyone else as productive and successful as possible. Everyone on the bus owns the bus. Collins wrote, "Letting the wrong people hang around is unfair to all the right people, as they inevitably find themselves compensating for the inadequacies of the wrong people. Worse, it can drive away the best people. Strong performers are intrinsically motivated by performance, and when they see their efforts impeded by carrying extra weight, they eventually become frustrated."[4]

> One of the most important *Whys* can only be learned from actual practice and that's *How* employee ownership will literally fill your bus with terrific people.

Every manager who ever lived can attest to this. But doing something about it, that is, getting the wrong people off the bus—especially with HR and Legal looking over your shoulder—is a whole bunch harder.

Collins even went so far as to recommend that "a company should limit its growth based on its ability to attract great people."[5] I wouldn't worry about this one too much. As you'll soon learn, employee-owned companies are magnets for superstars.

This is just one reason *why* employee ownership—especially 100 percent employee ownership—works. If there's a bad egg, it'll get cracked. It won't just come down as one manager's struggle—it'll be the force of many making it happen. Conversely, good eggs find themselves in good company, and that attracts like-minded individuals. Individually, the good eggs all benefit from the group's success.

One of the most important *Whys* can only be learned from actual practice and that's *How* employee ownership will literally fill your bus with terrific people. See chapter five for dealing with the "problem" of having more great people waiting at every bus stop than can currently fit on your bus.

And with so many people working toward the same goal, momentum builds.

2. Owners working together spin the *flywheel* faster.

What Jim Collins called the "Flywheel Effect," my home team KU Jayhawks would call "momentum." The tide turns in a game. Somebody makes a big three or, better yet, a great defensive play. The crowd rises . . . the momentum turns. Everybody picks it up and plays harder for as long as the momentum is yours. Whether basketball or business, it's all about momentum.

Success breeds success, and Collins's flywheel is the perfect analogy for how this works in business. "Pushing with great effort, you get a flywheel to inch forward, moving almost imperceptibly at first," he wrote. "You keep pushing and, after two or three hours of persistent effort, you get the flywheel to complete one entire turn. More hard work—another turn. Then another. You keep at it diligently, and at some point—breakthrough! The momentum of the thing kicks in your favor, hurling the flywheel forward, turn after turn—whoosh! Its own heavy weight starts working for you. You're pushing no harder than during the first rotation, but the flywheel goes faster and faster."[6]

Each turn of the flywheel builds on work done earlier, compounding your investment of effort.

This is exactly how it worked at Burns & Mac. In 1986, getting the flywheel to take even the smallest move required the entire savings of ten families—our Big Ten. Their employees—who didn't consider themselves owners yet (including one Greg Graves)—were not believers. They, for the most part, watched while the ten pushed. After year one, the stock price went down, and the flywheel looked stuck. It wasn't, but I remember thinking that I should keep my résumé current. I remember many who soon left. Most would regret it.

> There was no miracle moment or great CEO that made it all happen. It was the consistent force of many on the wheel that created greatness.

Eventually, the wheel inched forward. Many more of us jumped up and took our turns at the wheel. It never lurched forward; it just kept moving a little faster, bit by bit.

This is important: It wasn't any one day or any one push that made our flywheel spin. There was no miracle moment or great CEO that made it all happen. It was the consistent force of many on the wheel that created greatness at Burns & McDonnell.

Soon, our flywheel took off with a momentum all of its own, just as Collins would have predicted for us.

3. Leadership still matters.

With all this employee-ownership esprit de corps going on, you may be wondering how important the role of the leader in an ESOP is. It's a great question that finds its answer in understanding *Why* ESOPS work. So, let's get back to your personal *Why*.

From Collins's research, we know that the most successful CEOs—his "Level 5 Leaders" of companies that transformed from good to great—possessed a unique combination of strong will and exceptional humility. According to Collins, "Level 5 leaders channel their ego needs away from themselves and into the larger goal of building a great company. It's not that Level 5 leaders have no ego or self-interest. Indeed, they are incredibly ambitious—but their ambition is first and foremost for the institution, not themselves."[7]

When I read this in *Good to Great* the first time, it forced me to do some deep, personal digging. Let's be honest: There aren't many big-time CEOs in America who aren't also big-time Type A personalities—me included. We're success-driven, which certainly leads to a lot of gratifying pats on the back from peers and subordinates. Egos naturally grow, and pretty soon you might just start to think it was all thanks to you.

Here's some good news: An ESOP organization will constantly bring the executive back to reality. Every employee-owner's contribution makes success possible, not just the contributions of one person, even when that person is a really effective "Level 5 Leader."

Any CEO worth their own salt would hope to achieve Level 5 Leadership. I've been lucky enough to know a few—from serial entrepreneurs and small business owners, to some of America's largest corporate CEOs. It's always impressive to watch their firms outperform their competition year after year. Now just imagine a corporate culture in which every employee-owner seeks that same goal as each individual ego focuses on the greater self-interest of all—great for its clients, great for its communities, and great for its employee owners.

Ah, but there's a catch. This doesn't come about simply by creating the ESOP structure—it must be sold, and it must be sold hard. That's okay. Level 5 Leaders specialize in knowing *Why*. A trusted colleague of mine, Stephen Smith, CEO and chair of employee-owned Amsted Industries, explained it this way: "ESOPs are legally organized as Trusts. But that's not just a legal structure, it defines the nature of leadership in a spiritual sense: The leaders are trustees for all of their workers. When you know that bad and risky decisions will affect not only your personal status, but the long-term wealth and security of thousands of people with whom you work, including that assistant sitting right outside the door, you behave differently as a leader. You behave in a relationship of trust with your employees."[8]

Jim Collins is this century's best investigator of how executives can and should use their individual strengths for the good of any organization, whether for profit, for community good, or, as he and I collectively hope, for both. If you want to achieve his Level 5 status both individually and collectively, then employee ownership is the only logical finish line.

Why? Because Duty and Integrity Are Not Term Limited

Traditionally, corporate leadership and an independent board of directors hold the reins of power over any organization. Unfortunately, big gaps often split open between this leadership and the majority of workers in an us-versus-them dynamic in American companies—particularly public companies. I've personally served on many boards for a variety of different organizations and companies. Here's what I just can't stand: board members who dismiss the worker agenda with "my only duty here is to the shareholder—all day, every day—and to no one else." *They just don't get it at all.*

Of course, board members and shareholders as a whole have an absolute duty to the financial success of the firm, but their obligation in no way ends there. I believe that the smallest shareholder in the smallest mutual fund would also say that *we* have an absolute duty to our team—to each and every employee. *We* have an absolute duty to our clients and our customers—each and every one of them. And, finally (I hope I'm preaching to the choir here), we have an absolute duty to each community where we work, live, play, and raise our families.

There aren't many silver linings to the COVID-19 economy, but one has certainly been the acceleration of American corporations that suddenly seem to get it. BlackRock might be the most aggressive and successful financial investment firm in global history. They certainly have a decent percentage of my and Deanna's nest egg. You don't typically get to such a position by playing nice. But, in the midst of the pandemic, BlackRock CEO Larry Fink said, "Going forward, there is going to be a lot more focus on society, customers and clients, family, and employees."[9] I'll be watching.

The Benefits of Duty

You just won't believe how true this is within an employee-owned company until you're there, but here are three terrific *Why* benefits of a 100 percent all-in ESOP:

1. Employee owners will get it. They will understand that (as my construction president used to say) "profit is not a dirty word." In fact, just one demonstration of good faith by the firm—a better bonus, a bigger ESOP dividend, or a rising retirement account—will not only inspire more motivation, it will create what any CEO would love in any worker: duty.

2. In ESOPs, "being a great place to work" is not an option, it is a foundational requirement to make the business model work. This should take no convincing at all. If the employee is the owner and every owner is an employee, why would being a great place to work *not* be mission statement number one? We're going to explore this more in chapter five.

3. Best of all (at least to me), happy, successful employees build great communities! They invest their lives in their small rural towns and in their big metropolitan cities. They want you—wait—*they want their company* to take a portion of the firm's financial success (which is now their money) and return it to the communities where they live. And they want to give back to the country where this livelihood became possible.

Employees who are owners get it way more than employees and/or shareholders who aren't, *especially if they trust you.* This cannot be overstated. If they trust you, they will . . . keep reading.

> Employees who are owners get it way more than employees and/or shareholders who aren't, especially if they trust you. This cannot be overstated.

No Term Limits on Duty

If you're all in—and I mean full immersion in the ownership pool—you will get to the point where you will understand that your duty to the ESOP has nothing to do with today or even this calendar year. The Employee Stock Ownership Plan is not going away. *It will never retire.* It can and should be viewed as infinite.

Can you just imagine your change of focus when you don't have to worry about the quarterly earnings call? Or what every single decision and/or corporate announcement might do to tomorrow's stock price? If you're a family-owned business and considering an ESOP model, can you imagine not having to worry about each and every niece and nephew wondering what this quarter's dividend is going to be?

Thinking infinitely frees you. It frees your time, your energy, your soul (yep, I just wrote that because I mean it) to think about what's *best*, not just what looks good today.

> Duty and integrity are not term limited. When leadership understands this, tough decisions don't get any easier, but they often become very clear.

During the COVID-19 healthcare and economic emergency, the ability to think beyond the current year has been a bigger advantage to employee-owned firms than ever before. American ESOPs didn't have to focus simply on 2020 economic outcomes. They could focus instead on employee safety, client confidence, and long-term strategies. And when millions of employees across America were asked to work from home, I am certain the productivity differences between ESOP firms and their competitors will certainly reflect the employee-ownership advantage over time.

Duty and integrity are not term limited. When leadership understands this, tough decisions don't get any easier, but they often become very clear.

Why? Because Economic Growth Is a Good Thing!

Now, more than ever, economic recovery will depend on the worker. With respect to Jim Collins's counsel to only grow as fast as you can find great people, I guarantee you this: That's not going to be a problem. You do this right and the best people will be knocking down your door. The first year Burns & Mac was named one of *Fortune* magazine's "100 Best Companies to Work For,"[10] we were hoping to hire about 500 people.

We had 75,000 apply.

That fall, I remember calling my son at the University of Kansas School of Engineering on Career Day. There were almost one hundred different companies there manning their booths and looking for new graduates. He told me Burns & Mac's line was the longest by far, reaching to the back of the room and out into the hall.

So, given all that, will a 100 percent ESOP actually help you grow faster?

Back to the stats: Without any doubt, the data shows that ESOPs will outgrow their non-ESOP look-alikes, and 100 percent ESOPs will out-perform those that are only part of an overall benefit package. The 2000 NBER study found that ESOPs in America grew 2.3 to 2.4 percent faster than their non-ESOP counterparts and were less vulnerable during bad times—reducing staff by only one-fifth to one-third of the levels of their non-ESOP competitors.[11] An earlier study by the National Center for Employee Ownership, published by the *Harvard Business Review*, found that companies that make the ESOP changeover grow by an average of 3.4 percent faster post-ESOP.[12]

A more recent study concluded in 2020 by Carver Edison claims an even higher advantage when public companies use employee-ownership benefit plans. It found that, over a five-year time frame, public companies with employee stock benefit plans grew at four times the rate of those firms without the same benefit.[13]

THE OWNERSHIP ADVANTAGE ———

MORE LIKELY TO STAY	LOYALTY AND PRIDE	WILLINGNESS TO WORK HARD	ARE INNOVATIVE
5-6%	**12-15%**	**6%**	**8%**

Joseph R. Blasi, Richard B. Freeman, and Douglas L. Kruse. 2017.
Evidence: What the U.S. Research Shows About Worker Ownership.
In Oxford University Press Handbook of Mutual, Co-Operative and Co-Owned Business.
Oxford, United Kingdom : Oxford University Press.

And why is that? Well, it is not all that complicated. Workers who have a capital interest in the firm where they work are more committed to that place than those who don't. The research again confirms that this is true even when workers have a relatively small share in that interest. Executives who understand the drivers that separate losses from profits will recognize how small changes can make big bottom-line differences.

It is not difficult to argue that the American economy as a whole would benefit over and over again if ESOP popularity increased. American economists, not to mention politicians, debate constantly whether America is capable of above-average economic expansion again.

> It is more than possible, *it is predictable*. And, it is the American ESOP business model that can make this happen.

It is more than possible, *it is predictable*. And, it is the American ESOP business model that can make this happen.

And 100 percent employee ownership is perfectly aligned with our nation's economy and psyche—its aspiration is embedded in the American Dream.

Why? Because American Exceptionalism Could Use a Silver Bullet Right Now

I believe in the idea of American exceptionalism but only under the broadest of definitions. Yes, it began with Washington, Jefferson, and their revolutionary brothers founding a new nation. Political scientist Seymour Martin Lipsit called America "the first new nation,"[14] and because of it, we were able to develop our own unique American ideology. Jefferson used that ideology not only to rewrite the rules of governance in the interests of personal liberty, but also to create America's economic advantage accordingly.

Employee ownership is the clearest current tool available to this nation to continue that economic advantage and, as such, American exceptionalism.

In every era of our country's history, this ideological foundation has been reinforced. For me, President Abraham Lincoln spoke it loudest at Gettysburg when he called it our duty to ensure that a "government of the people, by the people, for the people, shall not perish from the earth."[15] It's crucial to understand that Lincoln believed this was an obligation to and for the American people, but also for America to be the preeminent example for other nations and their people.

We have been. And we are. Not because America is great in the superior, exclusive sense, but in the inclusiveness of its ideology. Its dream is for all people.

Across the planet, since the Constitution was completed in 1787, America has stood as this example, as other nations have sought to re-create the model we defined. Admittedly, for every modern-day Germany, Japan, and Australia, there have been failures in our efforts to export self-governance. Cuba, Venezuela, and most of Africa are currently opportunities lost.

> We have been. And we are. Not because America is great in the superior, exclusive sense, but in the inclusiveness of its ideology. Its dream is for all people.

Today, the opportunities have never been greater or the cost of failure higher. Authoritarian governments like China and Russia are trying (and often succeeding) to expand their political and economic influence across the planet. It's imperative that America engage all our traditional State and Defense Department strategies to counter this. More importantly, we must lead by example of self-rule, personal liberty, and the economic advantage of democracy.

It's time that employee ownership become an integral part of this model—this is the silver bullet. Even in some authoritarian-ruled nations, entrepreneurship is accelerating at unprecedented levels. America can again be the shining star by encouraging the ESOP model with our closest international partners. There are already signs of ESOP success in Britain and India, and an outpouring of ESOP demand in Australia, but so much more is possible.

America is currently renegotiating trade and economic aid agreements worldwide. At the same time, America has significant economic and tax revenue problems stemming from corporate flight. Employee ownership belongs right in the middle of all three discussions about creating even more bonds of economic friendship—not only between nations, but with individual workers across our borders.

Why? Because America Craves Economic Justice

If you believe that America has all the wealth fairness it needs, I might lose you here. I grew up right in the middle of the American middle class, and I consider myself to be deeply economically conservative. I believe wealth can and should be earned in America. But I also believe it could not be clearer that the current status of wealth disparity in America does not reflect the views to which a true economic conservative should aspire.

> At no time in our nation's history has economic wealth disparity so closely resembled the 1776 version of Europe our forebears left behind. We fixed it once. We should fix it again.

Daniel Greenwald at M.I.T.'s Sloan School of Management, Martin Lettau at the University of California's Haas School of Business, and Sydney Ludvigson at New York University found that from 1952 to 1988 economic growth accounted for all the rise in company stock values, but from 1980 to 2017, growth accounted for just 24 percent of stock value increases. Most came from "reallocated rents to shareholders and away from labor compensation" . . . that is, away from workers.[16]

Wealth concentration may be the natural result of all-out capitalism in an economy consumed with productivity gains, but it is in *no way* in the best long-term interest of our nation. In fact, I would argue that at no time in our nation's history has economic wealth disparity so closely resembled the 1776 version of Europe our forebears left behind. We fixed it once. We should fix it again.

So, let's work on that. There is a lot to debate here, I know, but let's start with the current state of things and work our way back to *Why*.

I won't pretend to know or offer possible solutions for what America should do about the non-working poor . . . especially in the post–COVID-19 economy; something between Ronald Reagan and Bernie Sanders should do the trick. I applaud those who struggle with finding and making the right decisions.

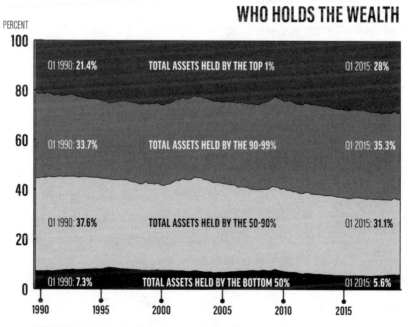

WHO HOLDS THE WEALTH

PERCENT

- Q1 1990: **21.4%** TOTAL ASSETS HELD BY THE TOP 1% Q1 2015: **28%**
- Q1 1990: **33.7%** TOTAL ASSETS HELD BY THE 90-99% Q1 2015: **35.3%**
- Q1 1990: **37.6%** TOTAL ASSETS HELD BY THE 50-90% Q1 2015: **31.1%**
- Q1 1990: **7.3%** TOTAL ASSETS HELD BY THE BOTTOM 50% Q1 2015: **5.6%**

1990   1995   2000   2005   2010   2015

SOURCE: FRED Graph Observations | Federal Reserve Economic Data
Economic Research Division | Federal Reserve Bank of St. Louis

But if we want to achieve economic justice in this country, a great place to start would be with "The Working"—that is, those actually employed and working for a living. I would personally love to see us begin with an honest, deliberate, and hopeful discussion about the minimum wage, but that's definitely the content of a different book. For this book, let's begin with the theory of *binary economics* when exploring how ESOPs relate to a more fair distribution of wealth.

Economic Equity

Binary economic theory was first described by political economist Dr. Louis Kelso. Some describe Kelso's theory as a bridge between Keynesian and classical economics, but it goes much further. Binary economics argues for the return of Jeffersonian economics to twenty-first-century America. Jefferson understood the nation's economic advantage was its entrepreneurial spirit. Kelso posited that same spirit is more than just alive today—it is also capable of creating greater economic expansion in parallel with greater economic justice.

> If we can simply create a corporate structure where we recognize each individual's working contribution not only as labor but also as an individual capital contribution, economic justice can be served, and capitalism can be saved.

Kelso's economic theory (some would say *agenda*) begins with the assumption that any individual has only two possible contributions to economic progress—their labor and/or capital. Kelso argued that as the world economies have become more and more capital intensive, primarily due to technological advancement, the contribution of labor has consistently been diminished. Worsening economic disparity was inherently soon to follow.[17] Kelso and his followers offered a solution that a few believe stoops toward socialism (or at least is too close to chance it), but I believe Kelso had it exactly right.

If we can simply create a corporate structure where we recognize each individual's working contribution not only as labor but also as an individual capital contribution, economic justice can be served, and capitalism can be saved.

Let me emphasize here that *"capitalism can be saved"* is not too strongly worded. In just this century, we have seen the problems of wealth disparity red-flagged in numerous other nations (many point to France as a perfect example). But even if eventual economic and political changes have worked toward greater wealth equality, they often do so at lower earnings levels. Being equal and poor is not the mission. In case you haven't noticed, there's a rising tide of anger even in our own country.

This is important: Binary economic theory never sought to guarantee that every employee owner get rich, but to *equalize* the opportunity for success—not just for the betterment of the individual, but for the national interest as well.

A good argument for both is the current American retirement challenge.

The Retirement Challenge

It's well documented that, currently, the average American working family is woefully unprepared for retirement. In fact, a recent Boston College Center for Retirement Research study warns that a majority of American households do not have adequate retirement savings.[18] Among that study's findings:

- Overall, 29 percent of all non-retired adult Americans have no retirement savings or pension.
- Worse, 48 percent of households aged fifty-five and older have no retirement savings. Among those with some retirement savings, the median amount is approximately $109,000—enough to generate only about $405 per month of income for someone sixty-five years old.
- Social Security—designed to replace only a portion of workers' pre-retirement earnings—is instead providing most of the retirement income for about half of households aged sixty-five and older.

In the post–COVID-19 pandemic world, this won't get somewhat worse—it's about to get *significantly* worse with a federal budget deficit dramatically less prepared to help. If we want to prevent an entire generation from retiring as big box store greeters, we had better work on this now.

Again, let's start by fixing this for The Working. Put simply, the traditional 401(k) program, or worse, defined benefit pension program, will not get this done. They are benefits, not strategies. Don't get me wrong; we had a great 401(k) at Burns & Mac, but it didn't and won't move the needle for the coming wave of retirees in America.

And don't even get me started on Social Security. A grand idea when it began in 1935 as part of President Franklin D. Roosevelt's New Deal, the legislation was argued to be "social insurance" for American retirees during the Great Depression, when poverty rates among America's elderly exceeded 50 percent.[19] Social Security has been amended numerous times since 1935, nearly always with good intention, but always with higher costs. It wasn't until 1983 that Federal Reserve Chairman Alan Greenspan led a commission study clearly showing the program could not support itself long term. Today, we simply ignore that Social Security is certainly "social" but in no way "secure."

> I was twenty-six when I came to this country from Ghana. I have been blessed to find a company like Burns & McDonnell thirteen years ago. I started participating in the ESOP the very first year since, and I also started participating in the 401(k), taking advantage of the full matching from Day 1. As at this writing, my ESOP account is almost three times as much as my 401(k). I am very successful compared to those I grew up with, not just career-wise but also the fact that I can breathe easy and not have to worry about my retirement. It makes it easy to focus on being excellent at work. Waking up to go to a "job" you can call your own has a huge psychological impact on your performance.
>
> —*Oko Buckle, vice president/general manager,*
> *Burns & McDonnell (Atlanta)*

In America, Social Security, 401(k)s, and pensions create non-poor retirees. *They have not and will not lead to economic justice.*

By their very definition, employee-ownership programs and especially 100 percent ESOPs can do the trick. Employee owners benefit to the extent of the firm's success and to the extent they contribute to that success. Large earners are maxed out by tax rules to guarantee that they don't swallow the program.

Finally, all win when the company wins. As binary economics dictates, employee ownership—especially 100 percent employee ownership—helps all employees create wealth through their labor *and* through their capital contribution to the organization. American economic advantage . . . secured. American retirement challenge . . . not solved, but much, much improved.

> In America, Social Security, 401(k)s, and pensions create non-poor retirees. *They have not and will not lead to economic justice.*

True economic justice in America should start with the creation of millions more American employee owners. They will get us on the right path.

Why? Because of Merrie

Merrie is exactly *Why*.

Remember Merrie from the Introduction? Merrie Ferguson isn't just perhaps my favorite employee owner of all time; she is, more importantly, the perfect example of why America should be encouraging more companies to become employee owned.

Merrie was a small-town American girl. Growing up, her family bounced from the farming communities of Dumas, Texas, to Goodwill, Oklahoma, until they finally landed at a pig farm near Merwin, Missouri. When others would ask her where Merwin was, Merrie would tell them it's just about ten miles south of Drexel, which didn't exactly help pin it down for most.

When Merrie wasn't helping on the farm, you'd find her where you'd find many rural American teens in the 1970s—the pool, the lake, the high school game. And as all kids do, she wondered what her future held. A little more than one hundred years ago, nearly one-third of all Americans lived on farms. Today, both the economics of farming and rapid technological advancement have dwindled that number to less than 2 percent. Along with so many others, Merrie left the family farm in hopes of a different future. What she wasn't dreaming of, not yet anyway, was retiring as an American millionaire and philanthropist.

With an associate's degree in graphics technology from Central Missouri University, Merrie landed a job at Burns & McDonnell making $4 per hour in 1979 when the company was still a division of Armco Steel. She was working on project instruction manuals for clients. A year later, I started at Burns & Mac as an engineer, making just a tad over $9 per hour. So, Merrie and I have known each other for a long time.

Merrie survived the company's massive layoffs of 1981 and 1982. She outlasted the Armco transition. She held strong through the first two years of employee ownership, when she strongly recalls, "We were scared but excited even as the stock price dropped in those first years."

It was about that time that I got to know Merrie better. She was asked to chair the company's new "Activity Committee" that had been convened to energize the rank and file. I didn't know exactly what that meant other than there were free doughnuts every Friday morning. But if you knew Merrie, you knew she could improve everyone's morale, even just a little bit, with nothing more than a doughnut.

I'm incredibly proud of nearly every aspect of my Burns & Mac story, but there was one event that still makes me cringe.

In the late fall of 1997, I had just been promoted to the head of the company's flagship Energy Division and was reviewing requested year-end bonuses and pay raises for the first time. Bonuses that year were easy to determine. We'd had a lousy year in my division, and our bonus pool was appropriately just as bad. It wasn't fun, but at least the math was easy. Raises were, for the most part, straightforward as well, with two exceptions: Merrie and another female drafter. Their base pay was not just a little but *a lot* lower than their male counterparts. I did not find the same problem in our engineering ranks, making this situation all the more blatant. I went to the bulldog, CEO Dave Ruf, and he agreed that it should be fixed and fixed immediately.

Merrie reacted to the news as I'd hoped. She was not only aware of the pay disparity; she had an opinion as to why. Most importantly, she was thrilled with the big raise and a better bonus than she was expecting.

As she recalled, "One day Greg came out and said, 'Hey, Merrie and Vicki, I just noticed you two don't make as much as the guys. Why is that?' We were like, duh, it's pretty obvious. And Greg stepped up for us. He had all salaries reviewed, then made them based on years of service, merit, the specific jobs you worked on as well as your attitude as you worked—your performance. That's how it ought to be."

Merrie's career blossomed. In her thirty-six years at the firm, drafting technology transformed engineering and construction firms from drafting pencils and T squares, to three-dimensional computer design programs, and now to virtual reality simulations. This small-town girl, who had also become a wife and mother, trained hard, worked even harder, and stayed current. Eventually, Merrie was training the firm's new engineers on the firm's design programs as well as managing a small group of her own.

And the employee-owned firm she loved was booming.

In 2004, my first year as CEO, I started a "Top 100" group made up of the leading shareholders in our ESOP. I typically met with them twice a year to present the company's detailed financial statements and answer questions. As you'd expect, the group was made up almost entirely of engineers. Imagine my joy when I called Merrie to my office the year before her retirement and welcomed her to the Top 100 group. I'm not sure who was happier.

The next year, Merrie took early retirement at fifty-eight. She and her husband, Ted, moved into their newly remodeled lake house in the Missouri Ozarks. Not only will she never be dependent on our federal government during retirement, she has become the successful career woman, mother, grandmother, and philanthropist any small-town farm girl could only dream to be.

"When you feel like an owner, if there was something that needed to be done, you did it," Merrie told me. "Anywhere else, someone might say, 'That's not in your job description—why did you do that?' Hey, I'd have done about anything they asked. I probably would have cleaned the bathroom . . . it was *my* company. The first share I got was $1. The second time

Merrie's dream home became real (2019).

it came around it went down. There were still major projects that didn't go and lots of challenges. But I was an *owner*, and if you acted like an *owner*, you were rewarded like an *owner*."

Why Not?

Why wouldn't employee ownership be the leading solution to the economic injustice and wealth disparity in our nation today? There were hundreds of Merries at Burns & Mac. And there are no less than 1,000,000 more just at the employee-owned companies in America today. We are only a solid grasp of *Why* away from that number exploding into a true nationwide egalitarian economy.

The examples beyond my personal experience are compelling. Here are just a few American ESOPs that have helped redefine our economy and nation.

Great American ESOPs

- Chicago-headquartered **Amsted Industries** is a monument to employee ownership. The company dates back to 1902 when it operated foundries for rail components. At one time, it was publicly traded. But in 1985, it was sold to its employees, and since 1998 has been 100 percent employee owned. From its start as a collection of foundries, Amsted has grown to be a diversified global company of more than 15,000 employees with nearly fifty manufacturing facilities around the world.[20]

- **Publix Super Markets**, America's largest employee-owned firm with more than 175,000 employee owners, posts a turnover rate of 5 percent for full-time employees versus a national average of 65 percent.[21]

- **W. L. Gore** is an 8,000-person, associate-owned company (they don't use the term "employee"). They are best known as the maker of Gore-Tex and famous for being one of the world's most innovative places to work. Gore is consistently named one of the best places to work in America, Britain, and Germany.[22]

- **Southwest Airlines** has both an employee-ownership benefit (although obviously not 100 percent) and a profit-sharing plan. In 2015, Southwest paid out $620,000,000 to its employees, adding over 15 percent to their total wages that year.[23]

- **Steel Encounters** is a commercial contractor based in Salt Lake City, Utah. For more than thirty years, the firm has been providing highly specialized architectural services, steel joist and deck, curtain wall, glazing, and more—the kinds of construction projects that require tremendous levels of skill and collaboration. The organization is 70 percent owned by employees.[24]

- After leaving Los Angeles in hopes of finding a healthier lifestyle, Bob Moore began experimenting with natural ways to grind grains and make bread in 1978. By 2005, **Bob's Red Mill Natural Foods** had an annual revenue estimated between $30 million and $50 million. In February 2010, Moore transferred ownership of his grassroots phenomenon to his employees using an ESOP. "This is Bob taking care of us," said Lori Sobelson, who helps run the business retail operation. "He expects a lot out of us, but really gives us the world in return."[25]

• The most famous individual story of employee ownership just might be Cathy Burch of **WinCo Foods**. She started working for 100 percent employee-owned WinCo at the age of nineteen and was a millionaire grocery clerk by forty-two. WinCo has been so successful that Cathy's store in Corvallis, Oregon, where just 130 employee owners work, has a combined $100,000,000 in their retirement balances.[26]

Clearly, Burns & Mac is just one example of the incredible results possible with employee ownership, but I must add that I believe it's a really good one. The process of growing from a small partnership, merging into a global empire, and ultimately becoming a 100 percent employee-owned enterprise put the *Why* of employee ownership to the test. That process had to succeed, or we'd all starve. But the right people, the right owners, made all the difference . . . people like Merrie.

What about the Merries in your company? Don't they deserve the same chance?

CHAPTER 3

WHAT?

What Is an ESOP, and What Makes It Work?

Good, you're still reading. I hope that means you've arrived at your own personal *Why*. Now it's on to some important details. Now it's time to tackle the "*What?*" You likely have a whole host of questions about ESOPs by now and here are some that I've had over the years:

- What exactly is an ESOP?
- What happened to get this all started?
- What was the first ESOP?
- What did Washington, D.C., do to help?
- What is an ESOP share, and how do I get some?
- What does a typical ESOP organizational chart look like?
- What is the fiduciary duty and, importantly, who has it?
- What happens if I have international employees?
- What kinds of businesses aren't conducive to ESOPs?
- What organizations are out there to help me?
- What are the pressing issues facing ESOPs today?

I have answers to all of those questions and more, so let's get started.

What Is an ESOP?

ESOP stands for *Employee Stock Ownership Plan.*

An internet search will get you this: An Employee Stock Ownership Plan, or ESOP, is an IRS-qualified, defined contribution plan that provides a company's workers with retirement savings through their investments in their employer's stock, *at no cost to the worker.*

For a more functional answer, I also asked the aforementioned Dr. Joseph Blasi, director of the Institute for the Study of Employee Ownership and Profit Sharing at the School of Management and Labor Relations at Rutgers University. His definition was so much better.

"An ESOP is a way for regular workers and managers to buy the company where they work without dipping into their wages or savings," said Dr. Blasi. "Think of it this way: When a real estate developer buys a building, he or she does not dip into his or her own pocket and use cash. They figure out what the rents on the apartments or stores will be and then they see if they can get a loan to buy the building with the rents paying back the loan. At the end, they become the 100 percent owner.

"An ESOP is just like that," Blasi explained. "Workers and managers set up a trust. They ask the existing owners of the business how much they want for all or part of the company. Then creating an ESOP is just a simple three-step process:

1. The trust figures out if the company's income can pay back a loan to buy the company. If yes, then . . .
2. The trust borrows the money from a bank to buy the company and pays back the loan out of the company's income. And now comes the good part . . .
3. As the loan is paid back, shares in the company are granted for free to the workers. That's it."[1]

Bob's Red Mill Natural Foods is an employee-owned firm out of Milwaukee, Wisconsin, that produces more than 400 natural, certified organic, and gluten-free milled grain products, billing itself as the "nation's leading miller of diverse whole-grain foods."[2] They also describe it perfectly: In an ESOP, the company sets up a trust fund, into which it contributes shares of its own stock or cash to buy existing shares. After an average of two years, all full-time employees participate in the plan. Shares in the trust are allocated to individual employee accounts. Annual stock allocations are made based on eligible pay. The ESOP provides a market for the shares of departing owners to motivate and reward employees. When employees leave the company, they sell their stock, which the company must buy back from them at its fair market value. Companies must have an annual outside valuation to determine the price of their shares. At Bob's Red Mill, their ESOP trust is managed by an external Trustee who represents all the employees.

The National Center for Employee Ownership (NCEO) estimated that in 2019 there were approximately 6,600 ESOPs in America covering more than 14 million participants. Of these, however, fewer than two million are within stand-alone ESOPs. Most of the rest live within public or closely held private companies and offer terrific benefits. Most are not the 100 percent employee-owned firms the nation would most benefit from. While ESOPs are found within nearly every American industry, manufacturing, professional services, grocery, finance, insurance, and construction make up about two-thirds of all participants.[3]

For the purposes of this book, and because I believe it's the only way to go, I'm touting 100 percent employee ownership. That translates to the company's stock being 100 percent owned by its employees *and*, even more critical, that 100 percent of the employees are participants in the program—not just a select few. They are all now truly employee owners, and that is entirely different than just having a group of employees who happen to own some stock.

Do you remember Manuel, one of our American Dream chasers from the Introduction? He's had the good fortune of being hired into a 100 percent employee-owned firm. Let's follow his employee-ownership journey a bit through this chapter so you can see what I mean. But first, an "Only in America" backstory.

What Happened to Get All This Started?

If you work at an employee-owned company and you love it, start by thanking the aforementioned Dr. Louis Orth Kelso (1913–1991). Like so many from America's "Greatest Generation," Kelso grew up during a robust period of economic growth in the 1920s, but what shaped him most was the American Great Depression and his service as a naval intelligence officer during World War II.

Kelso was an economist, lawyer, author, lecturer, and, you guessed it—banker. He is chiefly remembered today as the inventor and pioneer of the Employee Stock Ownership Plan (ESOP) that he developed to enable working people without available investment capital to acquire stock in their employer company and pay for it out of its future earnings. His most famous macro-economic theory publications, *The Capitalist Manifesto* and *The New Capitalist,* were actually not published until several years after America's first ESOPs were already up and growing.[4]

> ESOPs enable "The Working" people who don't have investment capital to use their company's future earnings to acquire their own stock in that company.
>
> —Dr. Louis Kelso

Kelso did not invent the idea of employees owning stock in the companies where they work. In fact, there were many successful companies in the early 1900s, both public and private, that relied heavily on employee stock ownership to increase employee motivation and productivity, among them such well-known names as JCPenney, Proctor & Gamble, Lowe's, and Pillsbury. Some of these companies provided stock ownership through

Dr. Louis Orth Kelso (1964)
"That's why the poor are poor . . . because they're not rich." –Louis Kelso

the vehicle of a stock bonus plan—another IRS tax-qualified plan designed to be primarily invested in shares of company stock. Sears and Lowe's, for example, invested more than half of the funds of their profit-sharing plans in shares of company stock.[5] Sears's plan was so employee-centric, former U.S. secretary of labor Robert Reich once described it as "admirably egalitarian."[6]

Kelso's theory of binary economics and his work to create American ESOP law changed the nation and the future for millions of workers. ESOPs operationalized the idea that employees could get a loan to buy their company and pay it back out of their company's future income. Their own sweat equity was the game changer, not only for workers but for thousands of American businesses that faced ownership transitions every year.

Kelso argued that transitioning or retiring owners of American businesses have basically only two options:

1. Sell the business outright to a competitor
2. Hope that the remaining executives can raise sufficient equity and qualify for the likely required bank loan

A third option—which in this author's opinion isn't really an option at all and is easily the worst tactic—was that the owners could just not let go. As a succession strategy, this one never works out.

Kelso's fear is playing out in America today. More than 50 percent of American small businesses are owned by someone fifty-five years old or older. And of these, less than half have a plan to transition the business to a daughter or son.[7]

Although he was sometimes accused of it, Kelso was not actually a democratic socialist. He believed earned wealth through labor should be more possible but that it should not be simply awarded. Kelso stated this firmly: "Socialism has been discredited. Plutocracy is in the process of being discredited. Democratic capitalism has yet to be tried."[8]

What Was the First ESOP?

In the literature, most have agreed that the first ESOP in America (they were then called Kelso Plans) was small paper publisher Peninsula Newspapers of Palo Alto, California. It might also be one of the most terrifying ESOP acquisition examples I can give you.

Kelso stated this firmly:

"Socialism has been discredited. Plutocracy is in the process of being discredited. Democratic capitalism has yet to be tried."

Peninsula's two founders, both in their eighties, had long believed that the company's own employees should be the logical buyers and the ultimate owners. Their employees were the ones who had made the business successful in the first place and the ones who knew the ins and outs of the newspaper business better than anyone else in the industry. The founders had seen too many of their competitors gobbled up by large chains and witnessed the effects of these acquisitions: key employees laid off and the identity of the company lost.[9] Kelso helped them create the first Employee Stock Ownership Plan in 1956 as a way to transition ownership of Peninsula to their chosen successors—the managers and employees of the newspaper.

But how could the employees possibly come up with enough money to buy the business? Peninsula was a highly successful firm and would not (and should not) go cheap. Actuaries gave them all the troubling news.

They determined that if employees cut their costs to the bone, borrowed all they could from friends and family, and mortgaged their homes to the hilt, they could still only manage to pay the interest, but never the principal itself on the unavoidable bank loan.

Risky Business

Kelso was personally invested in making this work. Peninsula's chief operating officer, Gene Bishop, had been Kelso's commanding officer in the Navy. The two dug in to find a solution. They noted that the company had for many years been making annual contributions to a traditional IRS tax-qualified profit-sharing plan, and that the accumulated funds were more than sufficient to make the bank's required 30 percent down payment. Granted, if these funds were used, the employees would risk losing a major portion, if not all, of their retirement savings. The workers believed, however, that it was certainly better than losing their jobs.[10]

One problem still remained—how to stretch the company's cash flow to cover the payments on the bank loan. One possibility was to stop making contributions to the company's profit-sharing plan, thus creating additional cash that could be used for debt service. That idea had obvious drawbacks. Then Kelso had a unique idea that altered the future for millions—including me.

Instead of having the company borrow money and repay the principal with after-tax dollars, why not have the profit-sharing plan itself borrow the money and repay both interest and principal out of the annual contributions the company was already making to the plan? Granted, the company would need to substantially increase the amount of these contributions, but as they were now an expense and, therefore, tax deductible, the net effect would be to repay both the interest and principal with pretax dollars. Projections confirmed that this structure would work . . . but only if such a transaction were allowed.[11]

There was one last problem, and it was a big one.

Nothing in the Internal Revenue Code allowed the leveraging of an IRS tax-qualified retirement plan. In fact, the 1954 code specified just the opposite. It stated that any borrowing by an IRS tax-qualified plan from the plan sponsor or other related parties was a prohibited transaction. The IRS Code did, however, permit companies to obtain an exemption from the confines of a prohibited transaction if, on a case-by-case basis, the taxpayer could prove to the IRS at the federal level that the transaction was arm's length and in the best interests of the participants.[12] The key here, of course, was who defines what is in the best interests of the participants.

Kelso secured the necessary exemption and fathered the world's first ESOP in 1956, although that term didn't come into common use until about twenty years later. Peninsula Newspapers made itself into the paradigm of an employee-owned company. Over the next twenty-five years, it prospered and paid out millions of dollars in benefits to its participants.[13]

Worth the Risk?

So . . . it can be scary. If you are now thinking that was way too much risk for the employees (make that employee owners) to take, especially in the newspaper business . . . well, I agree.

Thankfully, that one worked out; in fact, it worked out really well. Why? Because they wouldn't allow themselves to fail. Can you just imagine how hard they all worked? It might have been the first time in this nation's history that newspapers were delivered on time!

> Risk isn't always a bad thing. Employee-owned companies are in every way stronger in the long run if the beginning is a tough one.

As for new conquests into employee ownership, there will always be risk, but in no way does it need to be this high. Besides, risk isn't always a bad thing. Employee-owned companies are in every way stronger in the long run if the beginning is a tough one. It certainly was at my firm, and, without question, we were better for it. That's how it feels when you've got skin in the game.

Senator Russell B. Long of Louisiana (late 1960s)

What Did Washington, D.C., Do to Help?

Yes, believe it or not, sometimes Washington, D.C., does help! The Employment Retirement Income Security Acts (ERISA) of 1969 and 1974 are great examples. This legislation went a long way in protecting employee pensions and other savings plans in America. But it also posed a problem for the formation of ESOPs because of the self-dealing prohibitions. If we started this chapter by thanking Dr. Kelso, we must now extend our gratitude to Louisiana senator Russell B. Long (1918–2003), who chaired the U.S. Senate's powerful Finance Committee from 1966 to 1981.[14]

Long's senatorial résumé is filled with accomplishments well beyond ESOPs, including the first major expansion of Social Security, the formation of the Earned Income Tax Credit, the Child Support Enforcement Act, the provision for public funding of presidential campaigns, and the legislation that allowed the merger of the American Football League with the National Football League despite the obvious anti-trust concerns.[15]

Long was what I like to call a "Hubert Humphrey Democrat." He was people-first, but he was also a staunch capitalist. He took his fiduciary duty very seriously and, I believe, would have been perfectly suited to lead during the COVID-19 pandemic. In the face of a humanitarian and economic crisis, Long was known for swift action without a thought for his or anyone else's political future.

Several famous Senator Long quotes still ring true today, including the three below:

> I have become convinced you're going to have to have capital if you're going to have capitalism.

> Don't tax you, don't tax me, tax that fellow behind the tree!

> A government by secrecy benefits no one. It injures the people it seeks to serve; it damages its own integrity and operation. It breeds distrust, dampens the fervor of its citizens, and mocks their loyalty. (*This is my personal favorite Long quote.*)

ESOPs as Geritol for the Economy

For our purposes, Long's most important contribution was the day he secured legislation enabling the formation of new ESOPs despite ERISA laws. Senator Long even invited Kelso to Washington, to work on the amendment. After a now-famous four-hour dinner, Long declared that ESOPs would be the perfect "Geritol" for the American economy. What followed was six months of political maneuvering by Long that eventually resulted in the ESOP definition and its permanent exemption being included in the final version of ERISA.[16]

After Peninsula Newspapers, Kelso led many more companies to employee ownership so quickly that, as noted earlier, they became known as "Kelso Plans," and numerous national news outlets took notice. He even appeared in a PBS documentary entitled *Own It* and an episode of *60 Minutes* entitled "A Piece of the Action" in April 1975 with Mike Wallace.[17]

What Are the Differences in ESOPs from State to State?

State economic development offices are always looking for an advantage within the ultra-competitive marketplace for American companies, in particular for employee-owned startups. This will certainly multiply a number of times in the post-pandemic economy. Pennsylvania, Iowa, New Jersey, Virginia, Nebraska, Colorado, Texas, and Missouri have already passed pro-ESOP legislation, and many other states will be or are already looking to follow.

Signed by Governor John Hickenlooper in 2017, Colorado's law creates a revolving loan program to be operated by the Colorado Office of Economic Development and International Trade. It even requires that the office's employees be trained in the benefits of employee ownership. One of the bill's sponsors, Colorado state senator Jack Tate, said, "Anything we can do to encourage ownership helping facilitate getting folks on the path of wealth creation, I think is a good thing."[18]

In September 2016, the Missouri state legislature passed House Bill 2030. It provides a tax deduction on qualifying sales to Missouri-based ESOPs. Missouri Chamber of Commerce CEO Daniel Mehan welcomed the passage of the bill, commenting in a press release that it will "help ensure employee-ownership is a viable alternative when business owners decide to sell. Having more owners selling to their employees will help keep Missouri businesses locally held and growing in our state."[19]

In 2012, Iowa governor Terry Branstad said promoting employee ownership would be one of his administration's top three economic goals, and legislators quickly answered his call. Debi Durham, then the director of Iowa's Economic Development Authority, said "unlike out-of-state buyers, ESOP ownership was less likely to result in layoffs." Legislation committed $1.7 million in funds to the program.[20]

In June 2020, the Worker-Owned Recovery California Coalition advocated the California state legislature to include $10 million in the state budget to support education, technical assistance, and even forgivable loans to businesses that transition to worker ownership rather than close. "By supporting the transition of small businesses to worker-ownership, the state of California will preserve jobs and businesses, reduce strain on its social safety net, anchor community access to essential goods and services, and cultivate a new generation of worker-owners who have a say in their workplace and share in the profits of their work," the coalition wrote collectively in a call-to-action piece.[21]

California won't be alone in the post–COVID-19 economy in realizing that transitioning ownership to workers at thousands of American businesses will duplicate Senator Long's "Geritol" strategy nationwide.

If this isn't already happening where you live, laws promoting ESOPs and employee ownership are probably being considered for legislation or development agency action in your state. You need to know the status. If you don't know where to start, one of the national ESOP trade organizations is usually a great place to look. Keep reading for more about them later.

What Are America's Biggest ESOPs?

Employee-owned companies in America range from firms as small as five people to the supermarket giant Publix. Here are the top twenty-five ESOPs in America, according to the National Center for Employee Ownership:[22]

Rank	Company	Headquarters	Business	Employee Owners
1	Publix	Lakeland, FL	Supermarkets	200,000
2	Penmac	Springfield, MO	Staffing	27,850
3	Amsted	Chicago, IL	Industrial Components	18,000
4	Houchens	Bowling Green, KY	Supermarkets	18,000
5	WinCo	Boise, ID	Supermarkets	18,000
6	Parsons	Pasadena, CA	Engineering/Construction	15,000
7	Black & Veatch	Overland Park, KS	Engineering/Construction	11,600
8	W. L. Gore	Newark, DE	Manufacturing	10,720
9	Davey Tree	Kent, OH	Tree and Environmental	10,500
10	HDR	Omaha, NE	Architecture/Engineering	10,000
11	Graybar	St Louis, MO	Electrical Equipment	8,500
12	Schreiber Foods	Green Bay, WI	Dairy	8,000
13	Rosendin	San Jose, CA	Electrical Contractor	7,300
14	Performance Contracting	Lenexa, KS	Construction	7,250
15	Brookshire Brothers	Lufkin, TX	Supermarkets	7,000
16	Burns & McDonnell	Kansas City, MO	Engineering/Construction	7,000

Rank	Company	Headquarters	Business	Employee Owners
17	Janus	Lenoir City, TN	Security and Munitions	7,000
18	Burnett Companies	Dallas, TX	Staffing	6,500
19	EmpRes Healthcare	Vancouver, WA	Long-Term Care	6,200
20	Austin Industries	Dallas, TX	Construction	6,000
21	Gensler	San Francisco, CA	Architecture	6,000
22	Scheels	Fargo, ND	Retail Sporting Goods	6,000
23	KeHE Distributors	Romeoville, IL	Food Distribution	5,500
24	Wright Service	Des Moines, IA	Environmental Services	5,300
25	Terracon	Olathe, KS	Engineering/Consulting	5,100

What's the Right-Size Company for an ESOP?

The good news is ESOPs work for big or small businesses. Let's take a further look at a great example of a fully realized, globally engaged ESOP: Amsted Industries. As you may recall, this Chicago-based company dates back to 1902, when it operated foundries for rail components. At one time, it was publicly traded. But in 1985, it was sold to its employees, and since 1998 has been 100 percent employee owned. From its start as a collection of foundries, Amsted has grown to be a diversified global company of more than 15,000 employees with nearly fifty manufacturing facilities around the world.

If you see a freight train rumble by, look at those undercarriages (wheels, bearings, castings) and end-of-car connections—that's Amsted Rail. When a big, heavy-duty truck passes you on the highway, look at those end-of-wheel hubs and plastic interiors—that's Amsted's ConMet business. When a Ford or GM automobile pulls up next to you at a stoplight, beneath the hood are parts designed and manufactured by Amsted's Means Industries and Burgess-Norton businesses. And next time you're in a luxury hotel or large office building, or at an airport or a large industrial facility, you may very well be experiencing cooling provided by Amsted's Baltimore Aircoil business. You'll find those products all around the world, and it's the employee owner that's always at the heart of this success.

As Amsted CEO Steve Smith puts it, "It is the ESOP that forms the base of our culture of ownership that pervades our businesses worldwide. Employees have skin in the game and that makes all the difference. Why has Amsted been able to stay relevant in 'blue-collar' businesses that supposedly can't survive in America? We believe a big part of that is that our workers are owners. Even though the ESOP is a legal structure, the culture of ownership, respect, dignity, and trust that the ESOP culture promotes spreads throughout our businesses around the globe. Our mission is to keep producing lives of well-being for our workers by delivering premier value to our customers and our communities. That mission runs throughout the Amsted world."[23]

Amsted was America's third-largest ESOP as of 2019. But there are many more small ESOP success stories across the country as well. Kansas City's Global Prairie might just be the perfect example.

Global Prairie calls itself "one part creative agency, one part data analytics firm, and one part consulting company." It "unites the creativity, insight, and strategy needed to drive meaningful results." The firm was founded by Anne St. Peter and Douglas Bell, entrepreneurs who simply wanted more. One of Global Prairie's earliest clients, an employee-owned general contracting and construction company, engaged them to help build their marketing department. Their very first assignment was to help their client's employees better understand the power of employee ownership.

A decade after launching Global Prairie, advisors encouraged ownership to develop an exit strategy. Did they want to go public? Would they consider being acquired by a Madison Avenue holding company or a global consulting firm? Thank goodness for their people—ownership was more interested in an endurance strategy rather than simply an exit strategy. In 2018, Global Prairie became 100 percent employee owned.

And it shows: Today, Global Prairie is one hundred employee owners strong and has expanded to nine offices around the world with a client roster ranging from Global Fortune 100 companies, to entrepreneurial start-ups, to one of the world's largest and highest-ranked health systems. Global Prairie's employee owners donate 10 percent of all profits to civic, educational, and charitable organizations. And—my favorite—employee owners are given three weeks' paid time off each year to volunteer at the charitable organization of their choice. Global Prairie has a good *Why*.

What Businesses Are Ineligible for or Not Conducive to an ESOP?

I really hate answering this particular *What* since my personal experience always points to employee ownership as the best possible answer to many of life's questions. But since it's true, I will admit that even ESOPs have limitations.

Let's begin with the most obvious. An ESOP structure is not possible for the 21,995,000 federal, state, and local government workers (as of the 2010 official census).[24] But the good news for nearly all of these workers is that they already are, or can become, eligible for terrific (although some say egregious) government pensions. Compared to employee ownership, pensions do nothing to improve employee productivity (I would say just exactly the opposite), but they certainly do solve the retirement dilemma for many American families.

Employee ownership is also not conducive to the more than 10 percent of all Americans who work for nonprofit organizations.[25] Their work is often tireless and, in many cases, critical, but they simply can't be owners. For me, however, it's easy to also argue that several benefits of employee-owned companies could be translated to many of these organizations, depending on their mission, size, and their board's fiduciary appetite for pushing the envelope. Annual, long-term, and supplemental retirement bonus plans based on mission and financial endurance would be a great first place to start. For those really willing to challenge themselves, employee-ownership phantom plans might not be simple but would almost guarantee performance improvement. And, if every nonprofit in America operated with just 5 percent more effectiveness, just imagine how much better the world might get.

Within a few private and public companies, a historic but inane "code," or way of doing things, might hold some firms back—here are a few of the lamest excuses:

- Successful law firms can only be owned by the senior partners.
- Firms dominated by union employment can never get workers and management on the same page.
- Startups won't have the revenue and certainly not the income to make ESOP contributions when they're still utilizing angel-investor dollars (as an angel investor myself, I can assure you this is absolutely wrong).

However current ownership might conjure up these concerns, they should acknowledge the way the world is evolving right in front of them. They could absolutely make ESOPs apply in all these scenarios. With just a glimpse of long-term foresight, workers having a capital stake in the financial success of the place they work can create a positive, economy-saving, game-changing advantage.

Okay, I will partially throw in the towel when it comes to America's mega corporations. For example, it's simply not realistic to think that Alphabet, Inc. (Google) could finance a nearly trillion-dollar worker buyout over its 100,000 plus employees.[26] I'll give you that one.

However, in spite of Google consistently being named one of the (if not *the*) best places to work in America year after year, in my opinion, it can do better. Think long term: Why couldn't a 10 percent or even higher ESOP benefit be accumulated? Start big, Alphabet, but think bigger still . . . I'm just saying.

Dear Mr. Bezos,

Amazon is a terrific example of a mega corporation with ESOP potential. My wife and I are Amazon junkies; we have to be among your best customers—and you've got a lot of those. You're also employing hundreds of thousands of new employees in light of our pandemic-altered economy. A lot of people owe you thanks, but I'm sure you know that you owe a debt of gratitude right back—so why don't you start with your workers? Amazon could easily begin an ESOP benefit program for all workers—including part-time. It would lower turnover. It would improve customer satisfaction. It would probably help you buy another island or two. And maybe, just maybe, it could not only improve but *ensure* a healthy retirement for another million Americans.

Looking forward to your reply,
Greg Graves

Bigger Could Be Better

If we do wish to conclude, however, that megacorporations can't become 100 percent ESOPs (which I don't), then we'd have to take out the entire employment pool of America's largest employers. From Walmart all the way to McDonald's, approximately five to six million workers would miss out on the ESOP advantage.[27]

It may seem to you that we've now eliminated too many possible workers from an employee-owned future and that significant change to economic prosperity just isn't possible. The exact opposite is true.

In total, there are more than 132,000,000 unique, compensated, full-time workers in America today.[28] Removing all government employees, all non-for-profit employees, and, finally, all of America's top ten private employers, we are still left with more than 90,000,000 workers who would more than likely love to have their own little piece of the American pie. So, yes, there are a few places where this might not work, but the opportunity for better productivity, higher worker satisfaction, and greater economic justice should make even the most conservative economist see an American boom economy in the making.

And for these 90,000,000 potential employee owners, we will have taken a big step toward solving their coming retirement crisis. As the federal budget faces the daunting task of paying for the $5 to $9 trillion in economic stimulus (depending on how you count Federal Reserve action) needed to escape the COVID-19 collapse, this has become more important than ever. We simply cannot assume that recovering employment numbers post–COVID-19 will solve the retirement dilemma. Kelso called it "The Fallacy of Full Employment" in a world where there is a job for everyone, but not enough that create the opportunity for economic justice. I personally applaud the bipartisan actions in Washington for taking bold action, including those of the Federal Reserve. But

> Removing all government employees, all non-for-profit employees, and, finally, all of America's top ten private employers, we are still left with more than 90,000,000 workers who would more than likely love to have their own little piece of the American pie.

now the nation needs a revolutionary focus on American workers and their retirement wealth or we'll be facing another coming and exacerbated crisis.

Are There ESOP Failure Stories?

Of course, this answer is yes. Companies begin and fail all the time in America. That's capitalism. Sometimes, even older, well-established, and successful companies fail in America. It might be due to poor leadership or maybe it was just an idea that had run its course or got passed by. Again, that is capitalism by any definition. The fact that Sears and Lowe's are among the best early examples of employee profit-sharing exemplifies this important point: Employees owning stock in the companies where they work is not a guarantee for company success.

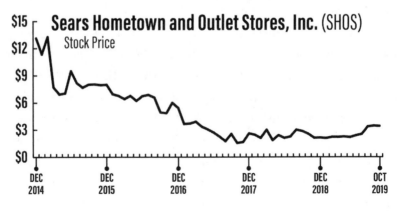

The *Chicago Tribune* and United Airlines are probably the most famous ESOP failures. In both cases, their partial ESOPs were simply not the fix for already difficult economic circumstances in troubled industries.

United was a particularly spectacular failure, resulting in its bankruptcy in 2002. The majority of its shares were owned by employees from a "benefit" ESOP program that began in 1994. Its ESOP was so poorly conceived from the start, I personally wonder if they gained anything at all:

- Only two of its three labor unions even agreed to be part of it.
- ESOP shares were actually traded for wage concessions.

Workers at United were immediately taking home smaller paychecks and, in all likelihood, did not "buy in" to being owners. Christopher Mackin, a United consultant at the time, wrote, "Employee ownership has become an empty slogan at United."[29]

Also, United wasn't the only airline struggling in the late 1990s and early 2000s. But its story serves as an important reminder that ESOPs won't fix a bad business plan or just an impossible set of economic conditions.

What Political Party Supports ESOPs More— the Donkeys or the Elephants?

You heard it here—the answer is *both*. Both parties are liking ESOPs more and more. The political philosophies of President Ronald Reagan and Senator Bernie Sanders couldn't be more opposite, but consider these statements:

- President Ronald Reagan: "I can't help but believe that in the future we will see in the United States and throughout the Western world an increasing trend toward the next logical step, employee ownership. It is a path that befits a free people."
- Senator Bernie Sanders: "Simply put, when employees have an ownership stake in their company, they will not ship their own jobs to China to increase their profits; they will be more productive, and they will earn a better living."

Economic conservatives like me believe that employee ownership is not anything close to socialism; indeed, employee ownership is the secret ingredient that turns American workers into capitalists. On the other hand, social liberals (also me) believe that employee ownership is also the ingredient that gives American workers more power in corporate decision making, improves retirement incomes, and nearly automatically promotes corporate transparency. *Both are exactly true.*

From the annals of ESOP's first Democratic cheerleader comes Senator Russell Long: "Bring on those tired, labor-plagued, competition-weary companies and ESOP will breathe new life into them. They will find ESOP better than Geritol. It will revitalize what is wrong with capitalism."[30]

> Employee ownership is the secret ingredient that turns American workers into capitalists.

And from the guy I wish would run for president, Republican senator Jerry Moran: "Employee ownership has a rich history in our country. The importance of ESOPs should not be understated. ESOPs boost wealth and enhance the dignity of workers who will have an even greater stake in the future of capitalism. Employee ownership allows us to reduce economic disparity and improve the financial well-being of our nation. Good politics and economic policy are combined in promoting employee ownership."[31]

A true economic conservative should support nothing more strongly than an idea that will make America more competitive, especially against totalitarian governments. A true progressive should support nothing more strongly than that same idea that will reduce income disparity and promote economic justice.

Convinced? Great, let's get back to Manuel's story.

What Is an ESOP Share, and How Do I Get Some?

Just to start things easy, let's say that our new employee owner Manuel works at the ideal debt-free ESOP company I've described that has one of the many legal ways to distribute shares in an ESOP. My experience at

Burns & Mac provides a great example. (ESOPs and debt will be covered later, don't worry.)

Technically, in an American ESOP, the ESOP itself owns all the shares in a trust. The employee owners hold retirement accounts within the ESOP trust that translate into their overall ownership in the company; that is, they own virtual shares.

In this model, new employee owners will need to earn cash into their ESOP accounts, which will allow them to purchase shares in upcoming years. How this works is that, at the end of each fiscal year, the company contributes, as a benefit expense, a cash contribution into the company's ESOP trust. That cash is then allocated into the individual employee-owner accounts, much as it would be in a traditional profit-sharing plan at thousands of U.S. corporations.

Which employees are eligible for an ESOP allocation can differ from one company to another, but as you'll learn in the next chapter, the most successful ESOPs are as inclusive as possible. At Burns & Mac, any employee owner who worked at least one thousand hours in that fiscal year and who was still an active employee on December 31 of that year received an allocation. The allocation method is simple and is subject to IRS rules. The formula looks like this:

> A true economic conservative should support nothing more strongly than an idea that will make America more competitive, especially against totalitarian governments. A true progressive should support nothing more strongly than that same idea that will reduce income disparity and promote economic justice.

$$\frac{\text{INDIVIDUAL COMPENSATION}}{\text{ALL COMPANY COMPENSATION}} \times \text{THE TOTAL ESOP CONTRIBUTION} = \text{ESOP ALLOCATION}$$

There's good news for wealth equality here, too. While ESOP cash is allocated based on total individual compensation, the calculation is limited by IRS rules that limit qualified retirement contributions, including ESOP cash contributions made by an employer. This is really important as it keeps the highest earners from gobbling up too much of the allocation and, eventually, the employee-ownership stock program. There is actually a second IRS provision that precludes or at least punishes ESOPs that "abusively" concentrate ESOP benefits to a "small number of persons." I don't say these words often, but *way to go, IRS*!

> The calculation limitation on high earners is critical to this working— not only from the perspectives of wealth equality and justice, but from the whole idea of employee ownership creating the highest possible company performance.

As a former high-earner CEO, I can't stress this enough. The calculation limitation on high earners is critical to this working—not only from the perspectives of wealth equality and justice, but from the whole idea of employee ownership creating the highest possible company performance. And, for the employee owner, it's all tax deferred.

Let's bring in Manuel and watch how his ESOP account grew in his first year.

MANUEL EXAMPLE

MANUEL'S ANNUAL COMP	TOTAL COMPANY COMP	ESOP CONTRIBUTION
$100,000	**$250,000,000**	**$25,000,000**

ESOP CASH FOR MANUEL

$100,000/$250,000,000 X $25,000,000 = **$10,000**

The company's ESOP contribution is, of course, a board-level decision. It does not have to be a specific amount or a calculated amount based on profitability each year. Most companies consider two separate strategies when making the annual allocation. The first is to watch stock repurchase liabilities and try to be certain that each year's contribution accounts for, as a minimum, the previous year's share repurchases from employee owners who retired or left the firm for any reason. The second is to try to keep the ESOP allocation to a consistent percentage of employee compensation. This was always my preference, but both strategies balance the ESOP contribution with the firm's annual profitability and will often result in terrific financial accountability over time.

Cash Versus Stock

Cash is nice, but even a new employee owner like Manuel can see that company stock is king. Each year in an ESOP, the amount of company stock available for purchase is going to vary. Any one year's available shares for repurchase primarily come from last year's retirees, quitters, terminations, forfeitures, and diversifiers. I'll discuss each of these in another chapter. If your firm has any level of success, both in terms of profitability and employee retention, the majority of shares will come from the previous year's retirees and will be straightforward to predict over time.

The shares available are now purchased by the individual employee-owner ESOP trust accounts with the cash the company just contributed, cash left over from previous years, and, with hope, company dividends paid to these accounts over time. Again, the calculation can vary, but most are based on a similar calculation used for cash allocation.

$$\frac{\text{INDIVIDUAL COMPENSATION}}{\text{ALL COMPANY COMPENSATION}} \times \text{SHARES AVAILABLE} = \text{SHARES ACQUIRED}$$

For Manuel, it played out like this:

MANUEL EXAMPLE _____

MANUEL'S ANNUAL COMP	TOTAL COMPANY COMP	SHARES AVAILABLE	SHARE PRICE
$100,000	**$250,000,000**	**500,000**	**$50**

SHARES PURCHASED BY MANUEL THIS YEAR

$100,000/$250,000,000 X 500,000 = **200 SHARES**

COST TO MANUEL'S ESOP ACCOUNT

200/$50 = **$10,000**

So, after his first year of employee ownership, Manuel's ESOP account now has two hundred shares of company stock and zero cash. In a well-run ESOP, his account will have more and more shares over time, of course, but it will also have more and more excess cash due to continuing ESOP contributions, the company's annual dividends paid to ESOP shareholders from net income, and investment gains made on that cash in trust (more on that also in chapter five).

It should come as no surprise that, occasionally, new employee owners might run out of cash in year one and not get their total allocation of shares, especially if employee retention is high. That is a great problem to have. In the long run, however, this works perfectly.

ESOP accounts typically become fully vested in five to six years after employment.

Can't the Company Purchase and Allocate Shares Directly and Avoid the Cash Accounts?

My good friend and former CFO Denny Scott helped me tirelessly with this chapter. He told me, "Greg, if there are almost seven thousand ESOPs in America, there are probably one thousand ways to operate them. The answer here is yes. Your firm can eliminate the cash accounts by simply purchasing all available shares each year as participants exit the company, and reallocate them to current participants based on their relative compensation for the year."

This strategy brings business cycle risk into the equation, which would need to be mitigated with structural safeguards. It also might preclude some really cool ideas I'm about to share with you in chapter five, but it certainly can be done.

What About ESOPs and Debt?

Most 100 percent American ESOPs, like Peninsula Newspapers, were the result of a thoughtful entrepreneur wanting to pass the company down to the management team and to their employees who made all that success happen in the first place. The challenge was always how that group could possibly come up with the cash to buy out the boss. Dr. Kelso and Senator Long to the rescue again!

Every four to five years, the federal government gives about a trillion dollars in tax incentives, tax breaks, tax deductions, and other tax benefits to businesses. If you want to encourage companies in this country to do something you want, to some extent you need to provide tax incentives.[32] Senator Long brought Dr. Kelso back to Washington, and together they figured those out for ESOPs.

Long built multiple tax advantages into the formation of the first American ESOPs that motivated the big three—sellers, buyers, and financers—to find ways to make these buyouts work. The key barriers to making employee-ownership buyouts reach agreement were often sellers not wanting to wait to get their money; buyers establishing credit and accumulating down payments; and, of course, banks must be willing to make ESOP buyout loans in what could superficially be seen as a high-risk transaction. You can read all about this in the previously cited article by The Menke Group,[33] but here are the high points:

1. Tax-Free Roll-Over Treatment

This provision granted a deferral of capital gains taxation for the seller if the ESOP acquired 30 percent or more of the stock of a privately held C corporation, provided that the sellers reinvested a like amount of money in stocks or bonds of other U.S. corporations within twelve months of the date of sale to the ESOP. And at the time of the earliest ESOPs, capital gains taxes were even more onerous than they are today. Without this provision, many possible sellers would have simply held on to ownership, trying to avoid the short-term tax. This cleared the way for many owners of privately held businesses to begin transferring ownership to the next generation of employees and managers without the current imposition of a capital gains tax.

2. Fifty Percent Interest Exclusion

This provision allowed a bank or other financial institution to exclude from the bank's taxable income 50 percent of the interest income they received on qualifying ESOP loans. This was a tremendous motivation to banks, not necessarily to make every loan but at least to study ESOP buyouts and to look for risk mitigation strategies. This provision did have a five-year sunset clause, but during those five years it had a measurable impact in stimulating increased bank lending for ESOP transactions.

3. ESOP Estate Tax Assumption

This provision allowed certain qualified estates to assume the estate tax of a business owner in return for the transfer to the ESOP of company stock having a value equal to the estate tax liability. This provision was revenue neutral. It did not reduce the amount of the estate tax liability; it merely transferred that liability to the ESOP.

A later bill, also sponsored by Senator Long, provided that an estate could exclude 50 percent of the proceeds from the sale of company stock to an ESOP from the deceased owner's gross estate provided that the estate tax reduction did not exceed $750,000. For those owners who failed or refused to transfer ownership to their employees during their lifetime, these provisions encouraged their estates to transfer ownership to company employees after the owner's death.

Important note here: Both of these estate tax provisions were also later repealed when the provision for the 50 percent estate tax exclusion resulted in larger than anticipated revenue losses due to improper drafting of that provision. The 50 percent exclusion was later repealed in 1996.[34]

4. Deductible Dividends

This provision permitted a company to deduct reasonable dividends paid on shares of company stock held by an ESOP provided that the dividends were either passed through to participants or used to make payments on an ESOP loan.

On their own, tax benefits do not make for a successful transfer of ownership, but they might just make the continuation of that company possible in the first place. Without them, a lot of American ESOPs would not exist, Burns & Mac likely among them.

Tax benefits also won't make you profitable, and that's exactly what you'll need to be to pay back the debt on your now-leveraged ESOP company. The employee-owners' shares begin in a suspense account and are released to the ESOP members as the debt is reduced and, hopefully, eliminated. These leveraged shares are released to participants at the original share price but have the opportunity to be worth more (or less) depending on the early success of the company.

The only real difference in the calculation of the annual share allocation when there is debt to retire is the introduction of shares being directly allocated to accounts based on the original debt of the buyout being paid down. The calculation change is simple enough, but the share allocations

> In other words: Those employee owners earned it. These "originals" pay off the company's debt with blood, sweat, and tears, but it's worth it. The greatest of company cultures is just on the other side of this mountain.

can be significantly higher during debt-reduction periods. While these original company employee owners can accumulate shares at an accelerated rate, early ESOPs often struggle with the burdens of debt.

In other words: Those employee owners earned it. These "originals" pay off the company's debt with blood, sweat, and tears, but it's worth it. The greatest of company cultures is just on the other side of this mountain.

As you just read, many of Kelso's and Long's federal tax incentive approaches were phased out over time as ESOP ownership transitions were blooming all across America. That's perfect. But today, in the early post-pandemic world, tax and other government-sponsored incentive ideas are needed more than ever and, thank goodness, are being debated nationally as well as in nearly every state capital. If small business is, indeed, the heart of a capital society, then saving every one of them possible through worker buyouts is a perfect match.

What Determines an ESOP's Share Price?

Publicly held stocks of American corporations are priced like most things in a free economy: via supply and demand. As a corporation proves its ability to produce profit and, importantly, to produce profits in the future, its share price will rise with rising demand. When macroeconomics turn for the worse, during pandemics and/or recessions, for example, prices will fall as investors pull back that same demand.

Sophisticated investors tend to evaluate public corporations based on their price to earnings, or price-earnings (P/E) ratio . . . a simple division of the corporation's share price to its earnings per share. The S&P 500 might be the most watched indicator of stocks globally. The S&P 500, as its name indicates, is made up of 500 leading companies and, today, actually comprises approximately 80 percent of the total global market capitalization. The price-earnings ratio for the overall S&P has varied with time and economic outlook, of course. Historical lows of 4.78 and highs of 44.20 tell you that investing is not as simple as many might want you to believe. For almost all periods, however, the P/E ratio of the S&P 500 has tended to average between 10 and 20.[35]

When ESOPs are used as benefit programs within public corporations, determining share price for participants is a non-issue, as the benefit simply rides with the performance of the firm and its P/E ratio as determined by market conditions.

At nearly all 100 percent ESOPs, the ESOP trustee hires a valuation consultant to recommend share price. Some ESOPs do this quarterly, but for most it's an annual valuation. Valuing the net worth of a 100 percent ESOP is not an exact science because the valuation consultant will need to consider last year's earnings (which is exact) and its belief in the firm's future potential for earnings (which is not). Some ESOPs use an estimated P/E ratio to determine or at least ball-park share price, but most ESOPs use a discounted cash flow method. In finance, discounted cash flow (DCF) analysis is a method of valuing a security, project, company, or asset using the concept of the time value of money. Discounted cash flow analysis is widely used in investment finance, real estate development, corporate financial management, and patent valuations. Like P/E ratio, the discounted cash flow method still requires the valuation consultant to make certain assumptions about the firm's future earnings potential. Valuation determination might be inexact (again, welcome to capitalism in America), but there are typically many comparable companies to the ESOP firm that are publicly traded in America, and all these will give your valuation consultant, your trustee, and your board a good basis for this determination.

What's the Difference Between an ESOP and a Worker Cooperative?

While similar to ESOPs, worker cooperatives have two distinct, fundamental principles:

1. The workers own the business and they participate in its financial success on the basis of their labor contribution to the cooperative.
2. Workers have representation on and vote for the board of directors, adhering to the principle of one worker, one vote.

In contrast, ESOPs can include all employees and all company shares, or only a percentage of employees, and they often, unfortunately, don't include all company shares.

Worker cooperatives are not new, but they are growing in popularity among the youngest of workers/entrepreneurs. In 2017, the Democracy at Work Institute estimated that there were fewer than 400 worker cooperative firms in America, employing about 7,000 people.[36]

Worker cooperatives tend to be more horizontal in their structure, with no internal hierarchy, and are often very small enterprises, with a few exceptions. Worker cooperatives are, by their very definition, 100 percent employee owned.

Here's your analogy: Worker cooperatives are like pirate ships. There's a captain, but they only have one share and are only as safe in their role as the next vote of confidence (or mutiny) of the crew. ESOPs are Alaskan crab boats from that TV show *The Deadliest Catch*. The CEO is the boss and calls the shots, but every employee shares in the season's profitability to the extent of their contribution.

What About Multistaged Buyouts?

There are numerous examples of multistaged ESOP buyouts in America. These often take place when a firm's current owners are convinced employee ownership is the right thing to do for their employees but aren't willing to walk away all at once. Another possibility, especially for larger corporations, is that the sheer size of the buyout may preclude the ESOP trust from acquiring all the acquisition funds up front. In either case, a multistaged ESOP buyout might be the perfect tool.

Multistaged ESOP buyouts are exactly what the words describe—a firm becomes employee owned over time. In fact, the final percentage of the firm to be owned by the employees does not necessarily have to be determined up front. As the firm generates profits, the ESOP trust can gradually take over a larger and larger percentage of the firm and begin the process of buying out the owner while building ESOP accounts and improving the firm's results through an employee-ownership culture.

One of the many keys to success here will be for the firm's leadership to balance the relationship between the declining ownership group, the ESOP trustees, and the highly motivated employee-ownership group.

Differences regarding valuation, compensation, and future corporate strategies are almost certain to occur and will have to be continually massaged if not circumvented. A better alternative for many might be for the transaction to occur 100 percent at the beginning but include a payout provision to the seller over a designated number of years based on the company's success. In this case, both sides win as the company succeeds. This provision is exactly how the Burns & McDonnell buyout with Armco Steel worked. Very specific wording should be negotiated between buyer and seller for this provision, however, so there are no uncertainties as the years go by.

What Occurs to ESOPs in the Inevitable Bad Year?

As you read earlier, bad years will likely be minimized by your employee-ownership culture, by your incredibly happy clients, and by your firm rising to the challenge of tough times. I'm writing this in 2020—the perfect example. Certainly, even the best of cultures can be victimized by the international economy. If your employee-owned company manufactures N95 masks, your firm was booming. But if you were a small restaurant in Manhattan, you had even bigger problems at home than at work, and no amount of culture was going to save you from a worst-case scenario.

Here's the good news: ESOPs have *multiple* tools to weather even the worst of times. Let's run through them now.

Performance-Based Pay Benefits

One of those tools that you'll read about extensively in chapter five is performance-based pay benefits. Burns & Mac is not alone here. Many if not most 100 percent employee-owned firms use performance-based pay as both the benefit it is intended for (to get financial results directly into the hands of your employee owners as quickly as possible) and for its risk mitigation provisions. Specifically, performance-based pay is a cost and one that can be reduced or even eliminated in poor economic years. This is also a "one for all" and "all for one" provision when model leadership is most needed . . . believe me, all eyes will be on you.

ESOP Cash Contributions

A second tool is the annual ESOP cash contribution. While not all employee-owned firms contribute cash directly to ESOP accounts, those that do enjoy wealth-creation benefits for their employee owners. A further advantage may be a significant economic lever during a bad year—this cash contribution can be eliminated in any calendar year or even delayed to a brighter future.

And if you're speculating whether ESOP companies qualified for the Small Business Administration's Payroll Protection Program during the pandemic, they do. In fact, for ESOPs with fewer than 500 people, employee owners were the very workers the PPP was designed to support. Figures aren't exact yet, but the National Center for Employee Ownership reported that 828 unique employee-owned companies had participated as of October 2020 and are likely prospering again thanks to the program. As I said, sometimes Washington, D.C., does help.

Rainy-Day Fund

Finally, the lever my former CFO Denny Scott and I used to debate just about every year was making excess contributions to our ESOP cash to build up our "rainy-day" fund. Denny was probably right, and thankfully we never had to pull it. An ESOP's rainy-day fund is simply cash already held in the accounts of employee owners. In some ESOPs, these accounts, as we've discussed earlier, are stock only. But at those ESOPs where employee-owner accounts are made up of stock and cash (from cash contributions, corporate dividends, and, with hope, investments of that cash), this cash creates the fuel to keep the ESOP working during tougher years.

For example, if the company is having a hard year and cancels its ESOP cash contribution accordingly, there will still be ample cash within participant accounts to buy out any participants who left the company in the previous year. The ancillary benefit here is the focus it brings to your current employee owners as their stock accounts grow.

Employee Ownership During the COVID-19 Pandemic

Talk about the inevitable bad year. All of America (and, in fact, the entire planet) had an absolutely lousy year in 2020. But it did provide the ultimate test case to the theory that the employee-ownership model will outperform the economy as a whole during weaker economic periods. I would call it the best such test since Dr. Kelso and Peninsula Newspaper created the first ESOP in 1956.

Thanks to the Employee Ownership Foundation, the Rutgers School of Management and Labor Relations, and the international powerhouse survey firm of SSRS, we know the results of this test exactly. Their survey included 247 ESOP Association member companies with at least a majority ESOP ownership and five hundred other firms constructed to be representative of U.S. firms, all with at least fifty employees.

The survey results were no surprise, I'm sure, to Dr. Blasi and his team at Rutgers. Furthermore, they clearly validated the American ESOP advantage, even during the toughest of times.

- Employee-owned businesses experienced job losses at a rate of less than 25 percent of nonemployee-owned firms.
- Sixteen percent of employees at ESOP companies saw their hours reduced, versus 26 percent at the other firms.
- Twenty-seven percent of employees at ESOP companies took pay cuts, versus 57 percent at the other firms.
- ESOP companies were more likely to provide, and were more thorough in providing, proactive pandemic protection, including a nearly 10 percent spread in taking protective measures. They also sent employees to work from home 85 percent of the time, versus 67 percent for other firms.

Rutgers concluded that, "The pandemic was a major shock for companies nationwide . . . the stark differences between ESOP and other firms was not in their recognition of the shock of the pandemic but their response to it." In the end, firms with at least a majority employee-ownership program had a higher outlook for the future, with only 1 percent of ESOP executives believing that their firm would not return to their usual level of operations.

What Is the Role of the Fiduciary for an ESOP?

Imagine being responsible—professionally, ethically, and morally—for the financial well-being of your company's assets . . . and knowing that the company's assets are owned by all your coworkers and yourself as employee owners. I've personally been in the position of having a fiduciary duty for a publicly traded company, a couple of privately held companies, a terrific private school, and multiple not-for-profits. None of these comes remotely close to being selected and accepting the role of a fiduciary of an employee-owned company. Accepting that fiduciary duty should not be taken lightly.

> None of these comes remotely close to being selected and accepting the role of a fiduciary of an employee-owned company. Accepting that fiduciary duty should not be taken lightly.

SES ESOP Strategies, one of the largest core groups of ESOP lawyers, consultants, and investment bankers in the United States, defines an ESOP fiduciary as follows: "Any person with discretion over the management or administration of a plan, or who exercises any authority or control over a plan's assets, is a fiduciary under ERISA. The ESOP trustee, or any other person or committee designated in the plan documents as responsible for making investments in company stock, is a named fiduciary."[37]

ERISA requires that plan fiduciaries act prudently and solely in the interest of plan participants. Three of the most important responsibilities of an ESOP fiduciary are:

- Securing a proper valuation of the stock. This is typically done annually but many firms do quarterly valuations.
- Assuring that the interests of plan participants are always protected.
- Approving all purchases and sales of ESOP stock.[38]

And, to raise the bar even higher, most ESOP fiduciaries in America are insiders—they work there. Boards with an insider majority are held to even higher fiduciary standards. And, actually, this composition is quite common for its advantaged efficiencies at ESOPs, but the higher standard of acting "solely in the interest of plan participants" is critical to remember.

In chapter five, I'm going to make the case that this is a good problem— a really good problem—but clearly still a big one. The fact that fiduciary insiders are held to even higher standards simply cannot be ignored. There are many great ways to manage the risk *and* the responsibility *and* the duty of being an ESOP fiduciary, but one thing is clear: *Fiduciary duty cannot be delegated.* It is yours . . . read on to find out who you are.

What Is an ESOP Committee? Are Its Members Fiduciaries?

In nearly every employee-owned company, an ESOP committee is appointed by the company's board of directors and is delegated the responsibility to oversee day-to-day operations of the plan. This committee is the ultimate representative of the shareholder, and it usually either directs the trustee on plan decisions, such as voting shares, or actually serves as the trustee itself. As is often the case, there are a lot of ways to approach this and a significant variance in the power held here.

There are no rules about who can be on the ESOP committee or how they should be selected. In many companies, the committee consists of members of management and/or the board; in some, it is just a single member of management. More participative companies get non-management employees involved on the committee, as minority or majority members. There's also no right or wrong regarding size of membership.

But it is crucial that the committee understands its purpose.

The extent to which the ESOP committee members are fiduciaries depends on the powers given to them. ESOP committee fiduciary decisions could include, but would not be limited to:

- Making decisions as to the voting of shares in the ESOP where the law does not require a pass-through of voting rights to participants
- Making decisions about investing plan assets in both employer stock and other investments
- Purchasing stock
- Selling stock

- Ensuring that the ESOP pays no more than fair market value or, in the event of a sale, that it sells for no less than that same market value
- Selecting qualified advisors
- Assuring that the operation and design of the plan complies with ERISA
- Moving assets from the ESOP to another plan

If one isn't careful, it's easy to underestimate how important all this is. The ESOP committee might not meet often. They might typically only handle what appear to be smaller administrative duties. But often enough, ESOP committees feel the big hammer of fiduciary responsibilities such as:

1. ERISA Compliance
2. Share Price Fairness
3. The Actual Voting of Shares

If you're a 100 percent ESOP (and I hope you are), this also means that your ESOP committee elects the company's board of directors.

Don't fool yourself . . . if you're on the ESOP committee, you're just about as *"fiduciaried"* as they come.

What Are the Distinctions Between the Company Board and the ESOP Committee?

Under the laws of most states, the duty of a board is to act in the best interests of the company and its shareholders—with a duty of care and a duty of loyalty. In many ways, that sounds and feels similar to the duties of an ERISA fiduciary—especially when the company's only shareholder is the ESOP. In fact, in

> Don't fool yourself . . . if you're on the ESOP committee, you're just about as *"fiduciaried"* as they come.

many companies, the board and ESOP committees might be made up of some or all of the exact same people. But the distinctions are important.

At first, the responsibilities of the board of directors look pretty standard:

1. Act in the best interest of the company
2. Set goals and objectives for the CEO
3. Set CEO compensation plan
4. Ensure CEO transition planning
5. Monitor and provide guidance on company strategies
6. Monitor company performance both short- and long term
7. Appoint company officers
8. Approve certain but typically not many corporate actions
9. Avoid or effectively manage around potential conflicts of interest

But it gets harder:

1. Hire the ESOP trustee (directed or not?)
2. Appoint the ESOP committee (insiders or not?)
3. Nominate, to the shareholders, new board members (insiders or not?)
4. Establish, monitor, and perform stock repurchase plan

No easy ones there. More on all that in chapter five.

What Does an ESOP Organizational Structure Look Like?

As is true for just about any organization, reporting hierarchy (and exactly who hires whom, who reports to whom, and who appoints whom) varies from one company to the next. That's certainly true for ESOPs, especially for those that are 100 percent employee owned. Here's just one example of how a 100 percent ESOP might be organized.

ESOP ORGANIZATIONAL COMPANY STRUCTURE EXAMPLE

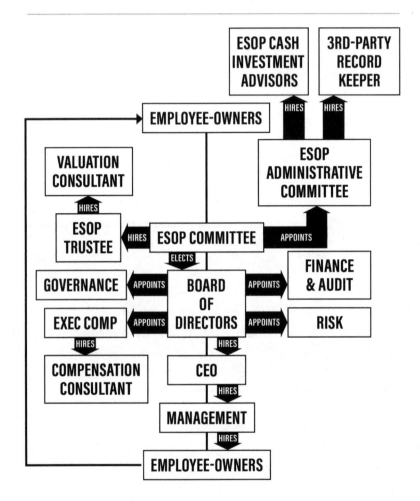

A couple of notes on structure here. Employee owners being at the top and the bottom of the organizational chart is important both structurally and culturally. On a day-to-day basis, employees work for management and, ultimately, for the chief executive, of course. But it's just as important to always remember the entire organization is established for the benefit of the plan participants—those same employees.

The board of director committees depicted here are typical but will vary from firm to firm. Some smaller or well-established larger employee-owned firms handle all business within the board itself and don't establish separate committees.

Finally, you will notice the level of separation between the company's board of directors and the ESOP's valuation consultant. This is a fiduciary must but does not mean that your board should not be intimately involved and understand what drives share price and, therefore, shareholder value.

What Are the Exceptions as to How Shares Can Be Voted?

Yes, back to Denny Scott's 1,000 ways. As you might expect, I'm highly opinionated on *How* it should be done. More on that in a future chapter, but it is true that there aren't many restrictions, and the possibilities are just about unlimited. Here are a few:

- Shares can be voted in total by your external ESOP trustee
- Shares can be voted by each individual participant on specific matters
- Yes, that's right, some ESOPs have the employee owners vote annually on board appointments, including the CEO
- Any combination of the above

But, while there might be unlimited possibilities, most ESOPs create a voting structure when they are founded and then stay consistent with that decision. The key is to stick with the duty of the participant. Then the best decisions typically see the light quickly.

What Is an ESOP Trustee? What Powers Do They Have?

Federal law requires that all benefit plans have a trustee. But for our purposes, it's important to know that there are expert ERISA trustees and then there are expert ERISA ESOP trustees. There is a big difference between them.

ESOPs must be overseen by an independent trustee who is under guidelines just as strict, if not stricter, than the fiduciaries of most other benefit plans.[39] ESOP trustees are:

1. Bound by the "exclusive benefit" rule; that is, they must act solely in the interest of plan participants for the exclusive purpose of providing retirement benefits
2. Charged to hire an independent valuation advisor for stock valuations
3. Responsible for setting stock price and making sure initial and annual stock valuations are done correctly
4. Held personally liable for mismanagement or losses in the ESOP

It can even be argued (although I really hate this) that the ESOP trustee alone decides how to vote the ESOP shares on the most critical company matters. This can change quickly, however, if the company's ESOP committee or board of directors opts to hire a "directed" trustee. See chapter five as well for my strong opinion on that!

It's important to mention that, in any regard, the ESOP trustee should be an absolute expert related to ESOP ERISA rules. They must have the ability to communicate clearly and effectively with the company board, a third-party administrator, the appraiser and valuation advisors, ESOP legal counsel, and all the employee owners of the company, if need be.

There is a long list of firms who act as outside trustees to employee-owned firms in America. They range from the largest and smallest of banks to law firms and even many boutique fiduciary providers. All the national ESOP associations have great contacts to most of these providers.

What Is an ESOP S Corp?

At any firm, an S Subchapter, or S Corporation, is a business entity that provides flow-through tax treatment to its shareholders. At many law firms, for example, the profits of the firm flow directly to the firm's partners who then pay income tax as individuals versus the company paying a business income tax.

The *S* in S Corporation stands for "small." There may not be more than one hundred shareholders and there may not be more than one class of stock. Fortunately for employee-owned firms, the ESOP Trust is considered a single shareholder regardless of the number of participants.

It's a model that can work very effectively within an ESOP. In fact, many 100 percent employee-owned ESOPs in America have switched from being a C-Corp to an S-Corp business entity for tax strategy purposes, including Burns & McDonnell (thank you, Mark) in 2002.

> When I started, we were about $110 to $120 million in revenues; when I left, we were at $2.8 billion. Employee ownership is the true key to this success. Burns & Mac has been an ESOP since 1986, and the biggest thing I accomplished when I was there was to take it to an S Corporation.
>
> Most publicly traded corporations (C Corp) pay income on their profits to the IRS. A law was passed back in the late 1990s that said to be an S Corp (which was formerly available only to individuals—and there was a limit on that) could extend to ESOPs. When you become an S Corporation, the corporation itself no longer pays tax. For example, if you were a C Corp and you had profits of $100 million, the corporate tax rate was about 35 percent plus state tax, so overall you were paying $40 million off to the IRS and state. You had $60 million in net value. By becoming an S Corp, if we made $100 million in profit, we got to keep it all. We would then pay dividends equivalent to the taxes we would have paid directly into the ESOP.
>
> —*Mark Taylor, retired CFO, Burns & McDonnell*

For a 100 percent employee-owned S-Corp ESOP, all income generated by the company flows to the single shareholder—the ESOP Trust.

Since the ESOP Plan is an IRS Qualified Retirement Plan, no tax is paid until the individual employee owners retire and their account is cashed out, similar to a 401(k). *The tax is paid.* Uncle Sam has his day, but the retirement treatment of the plan gives the firm and its employee owners the significant advantage of deferred tax liability perhaps even until they reach IRS-required distribution age if rolled into an IRA.

You might think, therefore, that every ESOP is an S-ESOP, but that's far from true. In fact, currently in America, only about 500,000 employees in 3,000 companies are part of S-ESOPs.[40] These companies have flourished in industries as diverse as manufacturing, healthcare, retail trade, finance, and construction. In March 2017, research by Matrix Global Advisors CEO Alex Brill found that S-ESOP job growth exceeded that of the private sector as a whole since 2002. Specifically, while total non-farm private employment in the United States has increased 8 percent since 2002, employment among S-ESOPs in continual operation since 2002 has increased an impressive 37 percent.[41] And data compiled by Ernst and Young's Quantitative Economics and Statistics (QUEST) practice shows that S Corporation ESOPs outperformed the S&P Total Returns Index in terms of total return per participant by an impressively large margin (62 percent), net assets of S-ESOP accounts in the aggregate increased over threefold, and retirement distributions to workers in S-ESOPs totaled nearly $30 billion from 2002 to 2012.[42]

What Organizations Are Out There to Help ESOP Businesses?

You're in luck. Employee-owned companies have a lot of friends out there working every day to help your company and your employee owners prosper. The ESOP Association, ESCA, and NCEO are at work in Washington, D.C., and across the country delivering for their member companies every day, protecting your interests, and making it easier for all of us to grow and maintain healthy ESOPs.

All three organizations have a ton of resources and plenty of people out there to help you navigate the ESOP process and stay current on the issues. Some may want a little of your money along the way and perhaps some of your time as well. I highly recommend your involvement in each. They are all easily worth your time and treasure.

1. The ESOP Association
The ESOP Association attracts more than ten thousand people annually to its local chapters and national meetings, including the annual Las Vegas

Conference and Trade Show, which is the largest ESOP event in the world. They are all about education, and they "believe employee ownership:

- Improves American competitiveness
- Increases productivity through greater employee participation in the workplace
- Strengthens a free enterprise economy
- Creates a broader distribution of wealth
- Maximizes human potential by enhancing the self-worth, dignity, and well-being of our people"[43]

Their meetings are terrific, especially for newer ESOPs. At most, the more experienced ESOP companies are always happy to share what works and what doesn't at their firms. If you attend them, you will very likely get to meet some of my friends back at Burns & Mac who regularly offer workshops and give insights into how our model has worked.

It's tough to beat their big annual meeting in Vegas, but I want to especially point out the ESOP Association's chapter meetings—this is where the rubber meets the road and where, I promise you, you will make your company better.

Just recently, ESOP Association president Jim Bonham said, "I think we're at a unique juncture in our country's history right now, and we're having a lot of debates about how the average worker can grow their wealth, where they can have a stake in what they do, and I think employee ownership is a solution for the tough problems facing the modern American workforce."[44]

In 1991, the ESOP Association helped found the Employee Ownership Foundation, which has operated in pursuit of a single overarching goal: to help more individuals become employee owners. The Foundation has raised and donated millions of dollars to collect data used by academics, encourage objective research, and facilitate dialogue about employee ownership between thought leaders. Going forward, the Foundation will also place a greater emphasis on raising awareness of the employee-ownership model among business owners and to fund more applied research that can further improve the market advantage held by well-run employee-owned businesses. The foundation is governed by a separate national board of trustees and is recognized by the IRS as an independent 501(c)(3) organization.

The last thing your organization will love about The ESOP Association is their variety of benefits to your whole organization. They don't just help at the executive level but all over the company: human resources, finance, government affairs, and legal.

Much, much more info is available on their website: www.esop association.org.

2. ESCA

The Employee-Owned S Corporations of America (ESCA) calls itself "the voice in Washington, DC, that speaks exclusively for employee-owned S corporations. Since 1998, ESCA's membership has grown to represent more than 160 employee-owned companies in virtually every state in the nation. ESCA company members engage in a broad spectrum of business activities and are a variety of sizes—from 25-person businesses to companies with 18,000+ employee owners—but all have one thing in common: A commitment to protecting the S corporation ESOP structure and promoting it so that more working Americans can become employee owners."[45]

ESCA's laser focus is advocacy in Washington. If there's a better advocacy group for anything in Washington, I haven't seen it. ESCA has greatly benefited from the leadership of political strategist Stephanie Silverman, who is a frequent speaker on federal public affairs. She and her team are as good as it gets. The perfect example was in 2017. As Congress hunted for ways to pay for President Trump's tax cuts, ESOP incentives were on the long list of possibilities but, in the end, went untouched.

The S-Corp tax designation by your firm will do more for the economic future, and therefore the economic justice, of your employee owners than just about any other decision you make—other than becoming employee owned in the first place. The folks at ESCA understand exactly this and preach it every day to the most important influencers in Washington, and, if you ask, they can help you do the same.

The ESCA website features policy updates that not only keep its members up to date on current legislation but provide guidance on what members can and should be doing—along with a continually refreshed list of key legislators. Although the 2020 event was virtual, ESCA's annual Federal Policy Conference creates the ultimate political opportunity to make a difference to employee ownership—not only at your firm but nationally. Don't miss it.

If you're an S-ESOP, joining ESCA is a must. This organization is single-minded and driven, as well as connected and effective. For more information, visit www.esca.us.

3. NCEO

While writing this book, I have lost count of the number of times I have been on the National Center for Employee Ownership (NCEO) website to confirm a fact, discover a new idea, or research an emerging topic. They are simply a seemingly endless source of knowledge for you and your firm.

The NCEO is an information and research powerhouse on Employee Ownership Plans that was founded in 1981. It has more than 3,000 members, ranging from employee-owned companies to consultants to academics. According to their website, "NCEO is the main publisher in the field, with over 50 titles ranging from issue briefs to lengthy books. They conduct dozens of webinars yearly and also hold in-person meetings around the U.S., plus a large annual conference. NCEO provides training, speaking, and introductory consulting, conducts surveys and other research, and have extensive contacts with the press, where they are regularly quoted."[46]

If you have an ESOP question, there are many places to seek answers. NCEO is a great place to start. A perfect example of NCEO's benefit to their members happened in March 2020. Within days of Congress passing the CARES Act in response to the COVID-19 crisis, NCEO had detailed information on the Payroll Protection program ready for its members, with specific applications and directions for ESOPs.

NCEO hosts a terrific live webinar series, where topics range from leadership development and succession planning to detailed finance and tax strategy. The webinar series should be key to anyone at the management or executive levels. These are not cheerleading sessions put on by former ESOP CEOs like me; they are specific how-to discussions that you won't want to miss.

There are so many publications and articles on their website, it might be daunting. Here are three of their best—search for them by title at www .nceo.org:

- "Creating the Ownership Edge at Your ESOP Company"
- "Red Flags in ESOP Transactions"
- *Employee Ownership: Building a Better American Economy*

What Are They Doing at Rutgers?

On March 7, 2018, the Rutgers School of Management and Labor Relations formed the Institute for the Study of Employee Ownership and Profit Sharing. Their study of binary economics and capital sharing, however, has been understood and expansive for decades. The Institute is run by my growing friend Dr. Joseph Blasi. While I am sure it is evident to the reader by now that I have Jim Collins fever, the truth is I have depended on Dr. Blasi and the research done by his team at Rutgers, often teamed with Harvard, for even more of the conclusions I have reached in this book.

For those of us who drink, eat, and sleep the belief that employees who are owners and owners who are employees will outperform their counterparts under virtually any circumstance, the work done by the researchers at Rutgers has been intensely gratifying. The Rutgers team has convincingly proven over the vast American economy as a whole what our lived experience has shown us in our own unique companies.

For me, the seminal work is *The Citizen's Share*. I hope Dr. Blasi asks me to endorse his next work in repayment for the blurb he gave this book. If so, I'd write, "In *The Citizen's Share,* my thinking that had developed through almost forty years of boots-on-the-ground direct experience was confirmed. Employee ownership is the answer . . . it's what we've been looking for to right the American economy." Thankfully for me and many others, Blasi and team proved the experimental hypothesis to be correct—at the national level, for the firm, and, ideally, for the worker.

But there's more help here than just the proof that we all happen to be right. According to Rutgers, "The purpose of the Institute is to study the various ESOP models that have emerged and will emerge of employee-ownership shares and profit shares in the corporation and society of the United States and around the world. The Institute studies approaches that broaden financial participation and inclusion in the economy and business organizations and allow employees to be fully engaged and share the rewards of their work."[47]

I've said this before, but I'll say it again: I highly recommend two of their publications, starting with the oft-mentioned *The Citizen's Share* and *Shared Capitalism at Work: Employee Ownership, Profit and Gain Sharing, and Broad-Based Stock Options.*

What Is the Role of the Compensation Consultant at an ESOP?

The management and defense of executive compensation plans are extremely important at any company, but they can be particularly tricky and must be approached at the highest fiduciary level within ESOPs. Of all the boards I've served on, none have presented more complex considerations than the particular fiduciary responsibility of determining executive pay. One reason is the often circular reporting paths within many American ESOPs, including ESOP committee electing boards, boards having a lot of insiders, and so on.

As with any public company, best practices for executive compensation in ESOP companies must take into account the standards established by Sarbanes-Oxley,[48] deferred compensation rules, and the S-Corp anti-abuse rules (if yours is an S Corporation), among others. You don't just need an expert, you need a highly defendable, completely autonomous expert who knows this turf. Enter the *compensation consultant.*

You don't need to read chapter five to know that hiring an independent compensation consultant is an absolute must, but the questions and choices are endless. At Burns & Mac, we treated our compensation consultant like our pseudo boss and continually shared plans and results. If he wasn't happy, nobody was happy.

What Are the Pressing Issues Facing ESOPs Today?

I don't remember the time exactly, but it feels like yesterday. It was about 2008, four years into my tenure as CEO of Burns & McDonnell. A United States senator was in my office. We were discussing the state of things at Burns & Mac. We discussed the economy . . . we discussed tax laws . . . we discussed politics. I was still a little new at this, but I was enjoying our chat immensely. Then the senator asked me, "So tell me, Greg, what can we be doing in Washington right now to help you?"

Now comes the part I do remember exactly. I said, "Oh, the best thing you could do in Washington is absolutely nothing."

Can you relate?

Without a moment's hesitation, she replied, "Oh, Greg, that's not our best skill set." How refreshingly honest, if not actually helpful.

My friends at the ESOP Association and ESCA, along with the Burns & Mac CFO and CAO, eventually got through to me that unless you are moving forward in Washington, you are likely falling back. I never said *absolutely nothing* again.

Given our nation's recovering economy and ever-changing political environment, there are not many issues on which the left and right can agree. Personally, I'm

> Given our nation's recovering economy and ever-changing political environment, there are not many issues on which the left and right can agree. Personally, I'm not sure how they ever could in light of the chasm that continues to grow wider and deeper with each election. But, as discussed earlier, employee ownership seems to have found just the right recipe to bridge the divide.

not sure how they ever could in light of the chasm that continues to grow wider and deeper with each election. But, as discussed earlier, employee ownership seems to have found just the right recipe to bridge the divide.

That's because employee ownership can make both sides happy.

- It grows the economy and creates jobs.
- It benefits each and every employee owner, not just the executives and owners.
- It almost always provides superior benefits, such as health insurance, personal time off, and higher education training.
- It reduces the federal and state government risk of burden by creating successful, maybe even wealthy, retirements.
- It creates great places to work.

I wish I had told that senator that *Washington should be looking for more and more ways to encourage more and more companies to follow an ESOP model.*

Legislation passed in 2018, the Main Street Employee Ownership Act, further encouraged the formation of ESOPs by facilitating transactions via small business loans through the Federal Small Business Administration.[49] It was a good step in the right direction.

The Small Business Association did make millions of dollars in low-interest loans to small employee-owned firms through the Payroll Protection Program. But now is exactly the time for much more. We should all be letting Washington know we can help America more (with or without the CARES Act)— much more—if it would simply encourage and promote ownership transitions to ESOPs in the near term.

> The time has not been this perfect since Kelso and Long first introduced ESOP-enabling legislation in 1974.

The banking system is ready, the American worker is ready, and with record-low interest rates looking longer and longer into the horizon, the time has not been this perfect since Kelso and Long first introduced ESOP-enabling legislation in 1974.

Within the time frame of the COVID-19 pandemic, a million Americans or more marched to protest the murder of George Floyd in Minneapolis. Proposals from the obvious, like renaming military posts named after racist military generals, to the debatable, like defunding police departments, created national discussion and, with hope, a measure of permanent change. An undebatable fact, however, is that the COVID-19 recession was the most regressive and racially divided in American history. Employee ownership will not, of course, lead to the end of racism in America, but it could lead to significant gains in economic justice through ownership share for Americans long marginalized for the color of their skin.

What Could Darken the Horizon?

There are some big issues being wrangled in Washington, today that might just affect ESOP success. They're not pretty. Some are just ridiculous. If you're serious about employee ownership, these issues shouldn't just annoy you—they should make you angry.

1. **Offsets:** Rumors are, congressional rules requiring Congress to "offset" the cost of new legislative actions with new revenue sources or by cutting a different federal program are milling about. At first, congressional rules requiring offsets seem like a great idea with deficit spending at the federal level continuing to skyrocket. If Washington is going to spend our money, they either need to figure out how they are going to raise more money, or they need to cut something else. Paraphrasing my friend the former U.S. senator again, *It's not their best skill set.* The big problem here is Washington tends to think incredibly short term when it comes to offsets, while employee ownership is a long-term play. Washington could at any time eliminate the S-Corp allowance for ESOPs and get a relatively small, short-term win *but a really big long-term loss!* We will be playing defense here. It is an easy choice for anyone who will truly listen.

2. **Qualified Restrictions:** I hate to say it, but this is an even dumber idea than number one when number one (offsets) is already as dumb as it comes. Another short-term revenue idea in Washington is to restrict

qualified savings contributions even more than they are today. The thought is that individuals of wealth benefit more than individuals of "less wealth" from qualified retirement programs. I guess that might be statistically true from one slanted view, but it is exactly what we should *not* be doing. The restrictions are already pretty darn low. As of this writing, they are limited annually to $56,000. We should be encouraging—not discouraging—Americans to save for retirement. I can't conceive of a better example of short-term thinking.

3. Finally, let's turn from tax policy to the **Department of Labor**. In my humble opinion (good grief, I'm pretty much going to make everyone mad now), the DOL sometimes reminds me of labor unions in America. Thank God we have them. They have made a tremendous difference on behalf of their members and employees everywhere, but too often they seem to be more interested in proving themselves to someone than in their members.

   Through their investigative and litigatory powers, the DOL is always trying to look for a spot where it can play the hero (have I made them mad yet?). And while ESOPs aren't their favorite target, the DOL has certainly discouraged some from establishing new ESOPs and has certainly made running an existing ESOP tougher and more costly. I'm talking about activities such as stock valuations, and so on, and I am thankful that the ESOP Association, ESCA, and NCEO are on our team.

Make no mistake, I am eternally grateful for the members of the United States Congress who, in many ways, sacrifice their professional lives to better our nation—especially in these times. I have lost count of the members of Congress I know who fly home (coach class, of course) every Friday night only to fly back to Washington early on Monday to be paid little and ridiculed big. I have met only a few I don't personally like.

ESOPs, and likely most issues, benefit greatly when U.S. representatives and senators think long term, and indications are that they can and will. Again, the Main Street Employee Ownership Act provides my best example. According to the aforementioned Drs. Blasi and Kruse, "In an increasingly rare example of bipartisan cooperation, President Donald Trump on August 13 [2018] signed a defense bill into law that included a popular provision that allows the Small Business Administration to straightforwardly loan money to employee-owned businesses that wish to buy out retiring small business owners. This and other changes in the provisions are significant. Not only could they double or even triple the growth rate of employee-owned companies over the next decade, we expect they will help stabilize jobs in local communities as well as reduce inequality by giving more middle-class families a means of accumulating wealth."[50]

With support from both sides of the aisle, including New York senator Kirsten Gillibrand (D) with co-sponsors Senator James Risch (R-ID), Chair of the Committee on Small Business and Entrepreneurship; Senator Ben Cardin (D-MD), Ranking Member of the Committee on Small Business and Entrepreneurship; and Senators Todd Young (R-IN), Jeanne Shaheen (D-NH), and Susan Collins (R-ME), the Main Street Employee Ownership Act altered certain government policies in favor of ESOPs.

Now, that's what I'm looking for in Washington . . . might we all be so thoughtful.

What About Manuel, Greg—Has He Retired Yet?

Manuel is about to retire—and even early at sixty. He never expected to or even dreamed of getting rich, but he was hoping that his employee-ownership journey would result in an economically safe and stress-free retirement. The math is simple, but I admit the truth to the following estimate is all in the assumptions.

In the graph that follows, the assumptions for Manuel's retirement are, in my opinion, conservative. If I ever meet you in person at an ESOP workshop, I'll share more possibilities for Manuel. For today, however, here were the keys to Manuel's success:

1. He worked extremely hard.
2. He worked like an owner because he was an owner.

3. So did the people around him.
4. And in the end, the place where he worked treated him like the owner he was, and he was fully rewarded for his labor and his capital contribution.

MANUEL GETS RICH ——————————————

ASSUMPTIONS

STARTING AGE	RETIREMENT AGE	STARTING SALARY	AVERAGE RAISE	MANUEL 401K CONTRIBUTION
25	60	$40K	3.5%	4%

	COMPANY 401K CONTRIBUTION	ESOP CONTRIBUTION	DIVIDEND RATE	SHARE PRICE
	4%	5%	10%	4%

- -

MANUEL'S RETIREMENT ACCOUNT

YEARS	401K	ESOP ACCOUNT	RETIREMENT
5	$33,000	$38,000	$71,000
10	$70,000	$105,000	$175,000
20	$190,000	$405,000	$595,000
30	$400,000	$1,100,000	$1,500,000
35	$550,000	$1,575,000	$2,125,000

7% ESOP GROWTH INSTEAD OF 4% = $4,100,000 IN RETIREMENT

What Else, Greg?

The most important final *What* might be, What is Manuel doing today? Fishing? Golf? Volunteering, perhaps? His retirement account, even in this conservative example, makes him a one percenter. What is he doing today? Whatever he wants to do, thanks to employee ownership.

There are a lot more *Whats* to explore, but this is a good start. If you want to become an absolute ESOP nerd, simply go to the Rutgers, NCEO, ESOP Association, ESOP Foundation, and ESCA websites, and you'll earn your virtual ESOP PhD in no time. You can read for days, maybe longer. ESOP conferences put on by each of these organizations and by the researchers at Rutgers can even give you more. I'll see you there.

Two big questions remain for us to resolve: *Who* makes for the perfect employee owner in your organization (it's certainly debatable, but I have the answers for you), and *How* can we turn employees into owners at your firm for explosive results.

CHAPTER 4

WHO?

It's Okay to Be Proud of Where You Work

Who are these workers we aim to transform into employee owners? For starters, never fail to remember that they are the most important part of every day for every CEO and for some very good and sometimes unanticipated reasons.

Best-selling author and business guru Dr. John Kotter runs Kotter International, a management consulting firm with offices in Boston and Seattle. He achieved international recognition as one of Harvard Business School's great thought leaders. In 2011, *Time* magazine listed his book *Leading Change* as one of the "Top 25 Most Influential Business Management Books" of all time.[1]

Admittedly, I may be favorably biased because Kotter's early path started like mine as an engineering graduate. We have at least a bit of common ground. When Leeanne Seaver and I interviewed him for this book, I was excited to ask him about many of his views on best business practice in the twenty-first century. Frankly, I was on the edge of my seat anticipating his insights on this book in particular.

Our conversation happened right as the COVID-19 pandemic was shutting the world down. At first, the discussion was so tangential I was praying that Leeanne was taking good notes and making sense of it (she was). Then Kotter started talking about a book he's currently working on that will no doubt be his next *New York Times* best seller. His points were spot on and solidified my thinking on the question of *Who*.

Kotter recognizes the potential for employee ownership to address the problem of economic injustice in America's economy. But I needed to expand my thinking, he told me. I had to include its advantage in the "leadership acceleration" future he's researching and why it's absolutely crucial in today's marketplace. He said that tomorrow's challenge of balancing corporate capitalization against equitably investing in our American workforce can be met, possibly even best met, through employee ownership. The key, he said over and over again, is to recognize that the importance of leadership is not just as great today as it was yesterday, it is accelerating explosively . . . as only an engineer could recognize.

The key is creating this exact leadership thinking and behavior in your employees. And that is exactly what ESOPs do.

I'll admit his validation got me literally right up from my chair, out the front door, and dancing in the street for the remainder of our call.

Who?

If you're going to even the wealth equation and give your employees full credit not only for their contribution to labor but for their contribution to capital from future earnings, then *Who* they are is the most important everyday challenge you face. And, if you will agree with me that the acceleration of the importance of leadership in the person, in the firm, and in this country isn't just rising, but rising exponentially, well then, you need to do this right.

In the next chapter, I'll give you my Top Ten Rules for ESOPs, but I'm admitting right now that there's a lot of *Who* in *How*. That's no surprise. *Who* is simply that important.

Unfortunately, *Great Employee Owner* is not stamped on an applicant's forehead in the job interview. But there are, fortunately, specific individual traits that separate the wheat from the chaff here—many your human resources department is already looking for, but each quality rises from important to transformational in an employee-owned firm.

Watch for the following traits when seeking to hire ESOP-worthy employees:

Financially Conservative

The best employee owners for your business are financially responsible on a personal level. You're looking for the kind of people who will treat the firm's money like it's their own (because it is). They tend to be fiscally conservative and are likely good savers. If they're not asking questions about the firm's business plans, 401(k), and especially the mechanics of your ESOP, be on alert. If you're a human resources professional and you're reading this, you might immediately worry about the job interview crossing into the inappropriately personal. You're right . . . this attribute is that important.

> Our country's founder, John Davey, came here from England. He was self-taught and hardworking. His first book about trees was self-published in 1901. He passed this company down through his family who kept that spirit alive. We became 100 percent employee owned in 1978. The history of our company is a living model of what employee ownership makes possible: We've survived through the hardest of times—wars, depression and recession, 9/11. Through it all, "We own it, we care" is what makes the difference. That's the staying power. Whether it's tree care in Arlington Cemetery or a small shop down in Florida, employee ownership makes the difference.
>
> —*Sandra Reid, Vice President of Human Resources,*
> *The Davey Tree Expert Company[2]*

Entrepreneurial

Ideal employee owners are often closet entrepreneurs whose low risk tolerance won't support starting a business of their own. Employee ownership can be exactly the right mix to quench their ownership thirst, while you've gained a terrific employee owner. I had a great boss who told me once to hire every former newspaper delivery kid I ever came across.

Your challenge here will be to convincingly sell your intrapreneurial culture within the firm—that you don't just allow it, but you encourage and expect it. Every great company is full of employees who think they could do it better and are constantly thinking about starting their own firm. You want that, and it's your duty (not theirs) to create the kind of company where they stay despite the urge.

> "[If you give them equity in the business] your employees will work harder. They'll recognize that they're an owner. They'll have a completely different perspective. And that benefits everybody. Now of all times, no CEO, no entrepreneur, can do this alone. You need every single employee committed to helping you get through this. Recognize that. Reward them for it."
>
> —Mark Cuban, entrepreneur, investor, and Dallas Mavericks owner[3]

Collaborative

Great employee owners are great collaborators. In my first week as CEO of Burns & McDonnell, I promoted a new chief administrative officer and a new director of human resources. That same day, Burns & Mac's current vice president of human resources, Renee Gartelos, became my director of recruiting. I remember congratulating her and telling her that she now had the most important job in the company (no pressure). I leaned on Renee for this chapter's attributes, and her first reply was "collaborators."

What a perfect attribute for you to look for in every job interview. It might seem difficult, but I personally think you'll find this easy to flush out with the right targeted questions. Collaborators usually don't care who gets the credit, only that the team won. So, when you ask about accomplishments, simply listen for the "I" word (red flag) versus the "we" or "team" words.

For my team, I want a quarterback like Hall of Famer Peyton Manning or Kansas City Chiefs MVP Patrick Mahomes. In interviews after wins, I have always seen them first credit their fellow teammates, coaches, and fans. Collaborators, more than anyone else, win over their teams and make them even more effective.

During the COVID-19 pandemic, ESOPs showcased remarkable responsiveness and agility. "Twin City Die Casting shifted production to make parts for ventilators and hospital beds. NewAge Industries, which makes plastic tubing that can be used in ventilators, has been investing in capital equipment, inventory, and hiring new staff. King Arthur Flour launched an initiative called 'Goodness Bakes' to keep bakeries running during financially challenging times. To that end, they've directed tens of thousands of dollars to purchase bread and other baked goods from King Arthur Flour bakery customers, which they then distribute to areas of need within their local communities—including food pantries, organizations that support unemployed food service workers, homeless populations, and more."

—NCEO employee-ownership blog on COVID-19[4]

Hustle

Great employee owners don't just work harder than their competition, they outright out-hustle them.

Here was always my visual on that hustle: Burns & McDonnell used to use an employee-owned printing company for large-batch engineering prints. Their truck would pull into our front parking lot, the driver would hop out, grab our order, and then literally sprint to deliver it to our front door. I'd stop what I was doing to watch that from my office window. It always made me grin . . . I absolutely loved it.

> Great employee owners don't just work harder than their competition, they outright out-hustle them.

Hustle reveals an important point about great employee owners. They hold themselves accountable to others: their clients, their communities, and their peers. They always take the call.

This might be a good time to again emphasize that employee-owned firms are predictably *great* places to work, but they are almost never *easy* places to work.

In fact, the best employee owners often take this to the limit and "ask for forgiveness, not permission" when there's a decision or an action needed quickly. I didn't always agree with but always rewarded this notion with only two exceptions: when there was safety or project risk. That said, I still rewarded it 99 percent of the time.

> In an increasingly divisive world, employee ownership engages everyone toward the goal. "We are all shooting at the same target. We are all aware of how close we come to hitting the mark. We all appreciate what is at stake: the equity—the literal dollar value—of the very entity for which we jointly toil and, therefore, the well-being of all those who depend on it. There is grand nobility in common sacrifice. We work with each other, yes. But the ESOP means we work *for* each other as well. And so we are unified."
>
> *—Todd Miller, vice president of sales for Essential Ingredients,*
> *a chemicals distributor ESOP based in Lawrenceville, Georgia[5]*

The Planner Type

If you tell me you've got your next three vacations already planned, or better yet, that you already have an Excel spreadsheet at home tracking your personal finances, then you, my friend, are hired. Successful employee owners are well-organized, proactive, long-term thinkers. This plays perfectly into how ESOPs pay off for their workers. ESOP accounts start off relatively small, but once your firm gets a long-term planner type to vesting (six to seven years), you'll have a highly motivated employee owner for life.

At the end of Burns & Mac's summer intern session, we would always have our "Night of Opportunity" for college students about to begin their senior years *and* for whom we were already making permanent job offers. Our department managers were always focused on the students, but a brilliant addition that Melissa Wood and Renee Gartelos made to that event was to invite parents and, occasionally, even grandparents. They always came.

I knew my job. I would happily spend time with parents at the ESOP Wealth Calculator station and, literally every time, I would later see those same exact parents put their arms around their kids soon after—whispering sweet dollar signs into their ears. Our summer internship program was so good that my part in it wasn't that important, but I loved playing to this key attribute of a great employee owner.

The takeaway: A key attribute of a great employee owner is the capacity for long-range thinking. Whether he or she comes to you straight out of college or elsewhere, the planner type is playing the long game.

> Investing in employee owners with on-going training and development is one reason ESOPs significantly outperform the competition. Those employee owners are developing skills that increase their competency and loyalty. In fact, ESOP companies are 1.4 times more likely to offer such training.
>
> —*The Employee Ownership Foundation*[6]

Financially Motivated

The best employee owners are not only financially responsible as noted earlier, they are also consistently financially motivated. They are not, however, greedy. Greed and ego are the two great killers of American companies. The best employee owners are neither. Greedy people, especially executives (and presidents), tend to be very short-term thinkers anyway. They won't fit it.

I do, however, want employee owners who are keenly interested in the financial success of their family, their project, their division, and, most importantly, their firm. They want to be part of a winner, in this case a financial winner. And, critically, they must trust (we're getting to the "trust" word soon) that when the company wins, they will win.

I'll admit here that one of my favorite duties was making the regular announcement of the company's quarterly dividend. It was very important to me that we made sure we had at least one but hopefully two long-time employees in every area of the building. I cherished hearing one cheer aloud when the dividend was announced, especially because all the new employee owners would hear it.

> "A 2017 report conducted by the NCEO with support from the W.K. Kellogg Foundation compared workers early in their careers, ages 28 to 34, with employee ownership to their peers without and found that being in an ESOP was associated with 92 percent higher median household net wealth, 33 percent higher median income from wages, and 53 percent longer median job tenure."
>
> —*OwnershipEconomy.org*[7]

High Expectations

The best employee owners have high expectations for the future, and they have them on many distinct levels.

For starters, I want them to have incredible, off-the-chart expectations of me as their chief executive. Leadership within an employee-owned firm is the highest duty, and employee owners should expect me to be brilliant, to hustle, to be responsible and accountable . . . and all the other qualities we are discussing here.

Employee owners should also have high expectations for the firm. Good employee owners aren't happy if they're just sitting still. No, I'm looking for those who think we should hunt down and slay the dragon. Even more important, I'm looking for employee owners who think that what we do here is important and worthy of an entire career spent making that mission possible. The bar is set even higher if you're willing to stretch what the future of employee ownership is in America. Those owners are looking for a firm that doesn't just do well, but uses that success to do good for others.

> I'm looking for those who think we should hunt down and slay the dragon.

Finally, of course, the best employee owners will have high expectations of themselves. I realize you can't hire 1,000 people every year who are 100 percent convinced that they will all be the company's next CEO (back to that ego and greed thing), but I do want them absolutely career- and purpose-motivated. If you're lucky enough to find a candidate who is 75 percent purpose and 25 percent career motivated, hire him or her immediately . . . you have a good one.

> Employee Ownership means that my best efforts have importance above and beyond my timecard. It ensures that my decisions and actions are continually relevant, not just for customers, but also for my peers and myself. This system helps to foster a sincere and meaningful feeling of community. I find this incredibly valuable as a motivator.
>
> —Tom Paluck, Customer Service Specialist, Bob's Red Mill[8]

The Engaged One (Not the A+ or D−)

As the saying goes, "Ds get degrees," but they also tell you a lot about the applicant's potential as an employee owner. Similarly, students with stellar A+ records may or may not be the right candidates. So let's consider the attributes of college graduates.

I remember it was the spring of my senior year at the South Dakota School of Mines and Technology. My graduating class from the Mechanical Engineering Department was small—thirty-three of us, all white, all male. It was small-town South Dakota at the time . . . you'd see much better numbers today.

Thirty of us had job offers, and nearly all of those thirty had already accepted positions and were planning their moves. The last three we referred to as "the D-minus guys." They didn't attend class often, and we never saw them in our study groups. Eventually, however, they did all get a single job offer just before graduation—from the same firm!

D− students don't make great employee owners, although I'm sure there's an exception out there somewhere. But here's the thing—from what I've observed, neither do the A+ students who never attended a college basketball game, never participated in club activities, or never went out for a beer with their friends. You should be looking for the graduate who has demonstrated acumen beyond academics, the one whose experiences are engaged in ways that tell you they not only have a strong IQ but a well-functioning EQ (emotional quotient) as well.

Give me the B+ sorority president or the B+ student who spent a year in Spain or even the B student who struggled with college at first but then fought his or her way back to respectability. The B+ student who had to actively hustle to get everything done, to learn good time management skills, and to fight to the finish line has strong potential. And if they've come through that with their GPS still on the bull's-eye, that grad is going to make a great employee owner.

> WinCo's employee owners are our greatest business asset and our most potent resource for growth. Our focus is on finding and motivating our next-generation leaders who want to make the lives of both

our customers and our fellow employee owners better with our low-price model. We want smart, motivated people who want to work hard, own the company, and take us into the future.

−Grant Haag, Chief Executive Officer, WinCo Foods[9]

Diverse

We simply can't continue to solve the same problems of this country with only those of us who have had all the same experiences. The overwhelming success of our nation's great melting pot experiment applies just as aptly to American companies. Great employee owners need to be a diverse group.

> We simply can't continue to solve the same problems of this country with only those of us who have had all the same experiences.

This begins with areas of diversity that are well defined. Employee-owned firms will be at their best if they see diversity as an attribute rather than a necessity or, worse, a requirement. If they can do that, diversity becomes so much easier to plan for and accomplish. Human resources departments do a better job of this when corporate leadership recognizes diversity as the competitive advantage it is. Be that leader.

Diversity takes many forms. Even if managers can override the habitual hiring of people who tend to look alike and reinforce the known formula, it can be even harder to bring someone on board who doesn't "think" the way everyone else thinks in the department. Breaking the mold takes a lot of proactive self-awareness. This begins in-house, of course, but it can and should quickly expand to firms hired for outside services.

Again, it's not just about ethnicity and gender; diversity is also about encouraging a variety of interests, experiences, and perspectives within the firm. And it's about living those values as an organization outside the firm as well.

You want a melting pot . . . that takes a lot of ingredients.

Florida-based Publix SuperMarkets, the largest ESOP in America, took a strong stand against racism and discrimination during the Black Lives Matter movement in June 2020, including a $1 million donation to southeast affiliates of the National Urban League. "With over 220,000 associates, we benefit from being an inclusive company made up of individuals who look and think differently, with backgrounds from around the country and around the world. Embracing our diversity has driven us toward progress, innovation, and excellence for almost a century. This diversity fuels my hope for the future, and all that we will accomplish by coming together as One Publix with One Purpose to care for each other with dignity and respect."

—*Todd Jones, CEO, Publix SuperMarkets*[10]

Believers (But Not Followers)

I remember a senior project manager our firm hired away from a rival. He had clearly spent a career believing that "The Man" had been doing everything possible to take advantage of him and pay him nothing. His attitude was really off-putting, and I thought we'd missed the mark with this hire. But I quickly got to know him and saw what a rare talent he had for project management. It became my personal goal to make him a believer in both our employee-ownership model and in me as a leader. I told him once, "I know you're trying your hardest not to like me, but know that I have always liked you." He tried not to show it, but I knew I had won him over the year he managed our firm's most profitable project and he was rewarded accordingly with a big year-end bonus. He said "acceptable," and we both laughed out loud. He retired as one of my officers . . . and I'm certain a true believer in our employee-ownership culture.

Belief comes from what's been proven, and, furthermore, it must be consistently demonstrated. This is another hard one to vet out during an interview process. You don't want someone who will drink just anybody's Kool-Aid but will fully intoxicate in your Kool-Aid once it's proven as their long-term plan for

> You want a melting pot . . . that takes a lot of ingredients.

> Employee owners who believe in their leadership, in their firm, and in each other won't just like the place they work—they will be undeniably, unabashedly proud of it.

success. Ronald Reagan's "Trust but Verify" notion might be the best corollary to what you're looking for.

Once earned, belief might be the most powerful weapon an employee-owned company can muster. Belief makes turnover a thing of the past. Belief makes client awareness—maybe even best in industry client satisfaction—an everyday advantage. Best of all, belief is the most important first step in being the best place to work possible.

Employee owners who believe in their leadership, in their firm, and in each other won't just like the place they work—they will be undeniably, unabashedly proud of it. That's why "believers" but not "followers" are exactly what you should be looking for.

It's okay to be proud of where you work.

Making this attribute a priority is critical, but it requires flexible and adaptive leadership from the top. You can't hire a bunch of independent thinkers without being open to what those perspectives are going to produce. Executive openness and honesty will create believers more than anything else.

> Working for a company whose leaders created a successful business and then turned around and gave it to the employees—who does that? I realize how special this place is, and I want to do my best every day.
>
> —Jason Lee, Facilities Maintenance, Bob's Red Mill[11]

Customer First and Focused

The very best employee owners are first and always customer focused. From 1987 to 1993, I worked for another Burns & Mac executive who saved my career. His name was Walt Womack, but we never called him anything but Wally. Wally was a KU Jayhawk, an electrical engineer, and, he would be the first to tell you, not of the highest GPA. Oh, but he was smart. I never met anyone who understood the difference between making a sale and creating a customer better than Wally.

Wally didn't assign me to sales opportunities; he assigned me to clients . . . eighteen electric utilities that the firm had never worked for before—in ninety years! My job wasn't to make sales; it was to create relationships and build customers. I remember one time we'd lost a big job in Indiana and my reputation inside the firm was so low people would avoid me walking down the hallway. Here's what Wally advised: "Go see your customer, Greg . . . you have nowhere else to go." I did, and that customer gave me a smaller assignment. I called it a pity award, but it led to more. And over the next few years they became our division's largest client.

You want employee owners who understand the difference between making the sale and creating a customer. You're not looking for Leonardo DiCaprio from *The Wolf of Wall Street*. What you do want is Tom Hanks from *Castaway*, who saved that single FedEx package for years and years just to make one customer happy.

In a job interview, observe potential employee owners for their listening skills. You want to know if they're *listening*, not just if they've heard you. Look for the candidate who doesn't simply repeat what you said but understands what you meant. It's a rare talent—never stop looking for it. This is even more important when considering promotions. There is nothing more frustrating or trust-breaking than a manager or, worse, an executive who is a poor listener. CEOs don't have to agree with their employee owners, but it is a requirement and duty that they listen . . . intently.

By the way, Wally was so good at this particular skill set (as well as steering people to their own best path) that he ended up managing the largest global practice in the history of the firm and earned a spot on my board of directors. He retired as the largest current shareholder in our ESOP.

When your employees are also your owners, everybody becomes a salesperson and every customer gets treated like a customer for life.
—*Walt Womack, retired officer and board member, Burns & McDonnell*

Owning It

Let me bring this back full circle to John Kotter's point about accelerated leadership. Great employee owners own it. They may not have the experience or expertise yet, but they've got the right attitude that will accelerate them through that process. They're ready for a world in which employees own that process and its outcomes. In fact, it's a world they will not only accept but may just demand of executive leadership.

Employee-owned firms are terrific breeding grounds for these exact kinds of future leaders. These companies likely already have a leadership development program in place, but the phenomenon of accelerated leadership increases the "need" and that "advantage" swiftly to the C-level suite. This is a perfect opportunity to bring in chief executives from other firms (employee owned, if possible) for think tanks and collaborative creativity. Let your people see the world accelerating right before their eyes.

For many, this will require pause and some deep thinking. I hope it does for you. How quickly can we respond to the changes that have happened? The world was already accelerating fast before COVID-19 stopped us all in our tracks (and in our houses). But the best economic minds in America are predicting that economic recovery will be full and fast but that business as usual is already dead. How will businesses function in light of everything that's going to be required of them in a post-pandemic marketplace? There are so many unknowns, but this much can be assumed: When your firm starts hiring, ask if the candidate in front of you is ready to "own it." You're going to need that mentality to keep everybody rowing in the same direction through the uncharted waters ahead.

Owners don't want today—they want what's well beyond tomorrow. They want and expect accelerated leadership from you. Maybe a better question here is are *you* ready for it?

> The rate of change has accelerated dramatically. Yet there are firms driving 60 miles per hour in a race where the world around them is going 100 miles per hour. That's not a good long-term situation— they're not going to finish well. We need people more engaged in the right way, feeling the urgency, actually helping—not resisting—change. That's totally consistent with the entrepreneurial mindset of an ESOP.
>
> –Dr. John Kotter, Kotter International and Harvard School of Business.[12]

Who Matters Most?

The research from Rutgers backs much of this chapter up for me: "We have a pretty good idea from the last two decades of human resource management research about the traits of an owner," Blasi states. "She would be a person who is oriented to taking personal responsibility and not just taking orders, who collaborates well with others, who is motivated to seek additional training and education in order to improve their ability to understand and solve problems."[13]

> Simply remember, the most important part of your day as a leader is *who*.

Simply remember, the most important part of your day as a leader is *who*.

The future of your firm depends on *who* works there. Are they employee-owner material—personally responsible and fiscally sound? Will they work their butts off? Will they think long term and have the highest expectations for themselves and for you? Are they smart enough, diverse, and customer-focused? Are they collaborators with leadership potential?

Can they believe?

Are they ready for the world of accelerated leadership?

In the next chapter, we will dig in deep, not just to finding the right people but how it works when everyone is working together to create something amazing.

CHAPTER 5

HOW?

Henry Bloch Gave Me That Patented Head Shake and Said, "Not Good Enough, Greg, Not Good Enough."

Wisdom takes time, experience, and often . . . outright failure. But sometimes, inspiration takes only a single moment. A lunch with Henry Bloch, co-founder of H&R Block, was one for me. The story is deep within this chapter and rings true to me still today. In the end, every decision leads you down another storyline. I am so fortunate that my path led me to a firm that would become 100 percent employee owned, and over my thirty-six plus years there would drill into me that without the right *How*, all the *Whys* in the world could be lost. I didn't always see them coming.

It was fall 1979, and Deanna and I had been married only a couple of months. It was my senior year at the South Dakota School of Mines and Technology, and we were basically (make that *actually*) broke. We even qualified for federally assisted low-income housing at $75 a month. Lucky for us, the coal industry was driving a hot American economy in the late 1970s. And that wasn't the only positive trend for engineering jobs. The military race with Russia was on; the space race to the shuttle program was on; an oil and gas boom, especially in offshore, was on; and multiple manufacturing industries were rapidly expanding as well. Deanna and I were getting multiple offers, so when a small engineering firm from Kansas

City showed up to do interviews, we didn't take much notice. Deanna and I already had great offers from California to Florida and back to Texas.

If I had known Burns & McDonnell was about to experience their Armageddon in 1981–82, I wouldn't have taken the job, and you wouldn't be reading this book. Looking back, I was more than a bit lucky to have survived it. But what I now know is this near disaster led directly to our firm becoming employee owned, and to me being an "original" shareholder in our ESOP. I was about to experience firsthand *how* an ESOP would change my life's trajectory over the next thirty-six-plus years.

An ESOP can change yours—and millions of others, too. Here's *How*!

Why? What? Who? Now: How?

American economic history is littered with incredibly successful (at least dollar-wise) companies that had no more *Why* than making the owner rich. But generational change is coming to America that will alter this course from individual to group-based economic capitalism and, even more important, today's worn-out model of economic growth without economic fairness will simply no longer be tolerated.

Today's worn-out model of economic growth without economic fairness will simply no longer be tolerated.

Of course, there are also many other examples, across our history, of firms with great *Whys* and who certainly knew their *Whats,* but followed practices not geared to *How* employee ownership can best be driven. In this chapter, we will dive deep in my top ten rules for how to turn your workers into owners for explosive growth.

1. Go 100 Percent . . . Stay 100 Percent
2. Hire Owners
3. In Fast, Out Fast . . . but Not All at Once
4. Diversify Them . . . Diversify Them Hard
5. Be Employee Owned, Not Employee Run

6. Profit Is Not a Dirty Word
7. Communication Rules
8. Implement Performance-Based Pay
9. Get Your Oversight Right
10. Be the Best Place to Work

Greg's Top Ten Rules for ESOPs

Rule 1: Go 100 Percent . . . Stay 100 Percent

Your firm is not a 100 percent ESOP? We better start at the top then.

The quantum leap advantage can only come when you accept the fact that your 20 percent ESOP benefit program is just that: a benefit. It's a good one, I agree, but you are not, in my view, *genuinely* employee owned, and thus, you will not experience the ultimate advantages of being an ESOP. You're allowing your employees to have some stock, that's about it.

To do this right, you've got to go all in, 100 percent in, and you have to do it twice. Specifically, 100 percent of the stock needs to be owned by employees *and* 100 percent of all eligible employees need to be included in your ESOP as owners. And if you are a lot less than the second 100 percent, you are just a glorified partnership.

It is perfectly okay for an entrepreneurial founder to keep a large share of the company's stock during an ownership transition as long as they are still working (*still working* is the key here). It's also a terrific idea if new executives are asked to purchase shares outside the ESOP to keep them focused on the long-term value of the shareholder, especially if they come from outside the firm. I'd never allow that to account for more than a few percentage points of all shares, but it can be a powerful performance tool.

You won't be *giving* away the company immediately in any event; your employees have to *earn* it over time. Just don't forget, they're not buying ESOP shares with their own money; they are virtually buying shares out of the company's earnings and/or its future earnings. A deep-rooted employee-ownership culture can only occur as the employees become employee owners over time. They must *earn* it and, even more important, they must believe in their gut that they've earned it.

Economic justice in America can't be the product of *given*. Given won't lead to any American advantage. Advantage will come from the product of *earned*.

So, no, I'm not saying you load people's accounts up on day one. They have to earn cash over their first year (more on that later in this chapter), buy their first stock in their second year, and so on. And, employees should be required to vest (a benefit an employee is only due after a specified employment period) over the maximum allowed time period—probably five to six years. After all, employee ownership is a retirement program. Moreover, it is an IRS-qualified retirement program with strict guidelines that actually work in your favor here. You're looking for lifers. ESOPs are exactly designed for that.

> Economic justice in America can't be the product of *given*. Given won't lead to any American advantage. Advantage will come from the product of *earned*.

What you'll find, I promise, is, once employees vest, they will take the final, critical, psychological leap to becoming employee owners. You will see your employee productivity soar and turnover rates plummet—every company's dream. I remember being invited to department "vesting" parties when an employee owner would hit that target. We celebrated them . . . and ourselves.

If you go 100 percent, your employees are going to stay—maybe even 100 percent of them.

Research backs this up even at public companies that employ profit-sharing, partial employee-ownership benefits, and/or stock options. Data collected by the National Bureau of Economic Research, the General Social Survey, and independent research by Rutgers University indicates that employees are significantly more likely to stay at the firm where they work when a capital interest benefit program is in place.[1]

Now imagine the difference you can make happen at your 100 percent employee-owned ESOP. Vested employee owners can quickly become employees for life—not so that you can take advantage of them, but so that you can feel free to invest in them without risk. What an enormous corporate advantage.

At Burns & Mac, low senior employee turnover rates added significantly to our bottom line. Not counting retirements, we had years where senior employee-owner turnover rates were virtually zero, or as close as you could possibly get. Given the often used notion that it "costs six to nine months' salary on average" and that "losing a salaried employee can cost as much as twice their annual salary, especially for a high-earner or executive-level employees," and considering the national average rate of turnover in America is 10 to 15 percent, *and* you can reduce that by even half, well . . . you do the math. A study sponsored by the ESOP Foundation suggests you should be able to achieve 6 percent turnover if you're just average at this.[2]

> If you go 100 percent, your employees are going to stay— maybe even 100 percent of them.

Another great American example is Publix Super Markets. As I pointed out in chapter two, the famed grocery store is 100 percent employee owned with an average turnover of 5 percent. Compare that to the industry average of 65 percent turnover. Incredible! And *Fortune* magazine ranked Publix number twelve on its "Best Places to Work in America" list for 2019.[3]

Is it any surprise, then, that Publix looked beyond itself during the COVID-19 health crisis? Publix employee owners did what they do best—made possible what seemed impossible. They developed a new initiative that connected Florida produce farmers and southeastern dairy farmers with Feeding America food banks to provide fresh fruits, vegetables, and milk to feed insecure households. More than one million pounds of produce and one hundred thousand gallons of milk were donated in their seven-state operating area during just the first two weeks of the effort.[4]

That's what happens when employees think like owners who are, in turn, thinking like members of the broader community. In the future, when people ask you about *your* ESOP, I hope you can begin just like

I always did. "Well, first of all, every owner is an employee and every employee is an owner . . . 100 percent of us."

What About International Employees?

Do you have a significant number of international employees? I did. Many countries either don't allow an employee-ownership model, have statutory pension structures, immediately tax benefits, or even disallow certain benefit expenses. This is clearly a problem for some of you. Don't give up easily.

Economic disparity is not just an American issue. In fact, it is far more prevalent globally. I would start by doing everything in my power to create a "parallel benefit" for every employee not in the United States so that the net benefit to each of them (and to the firm) is the same. In other words, make them virtual.

Retirement versus job security incentives vary widely from country to country, so do your research and don't be afraid to talk directly to your people. If parallel benefits are just not possible, then, unfortunately, you will need to accept the fact that your international employees are basically contract employees. That's too bad, but again, don't give up completely. Productivity gains, worker satisfaction, and other advantages found within an employee-ownership model are still viable, but you will need to look to entirely unique approaches for their productivity and career satisfaction.

Rule 2: Hire Owners

Certainly, at any firm, it's all about the people. Now multiply that times two for a 100 percent employee-owned firm. We're not just looking for the best *people*; we're looking for the best *owners*. And you need the best board members and trustees, too. If I told you that every person you hire for your firm is going to stay there forever, wouldn't you look harder for exactly the right one—no matter how bad you need them? You would examine every detail.

Remember this—your worst hire of every year is invariably the least likely to ever leave. It's time to raise the bar. From chapter four, you know *Who* you're looking for—so here's *How* to find and keep them.

Recruit Strategically: Don't Send Human Resources Solo

With apologies to three of my best friends—one who runs the human resources department at Burns & Mac, and two who used to—don't send human resources alone to do your recruiting. HR professionals have a critical role, but my recommendation is to send with them your best and brightest "product type" peers/employee owners to do your recruiting, especially on college campuses. They know exactly what you're looking for because *they are exactly what you're looking for.* Now give your HR recruiting experts the ultimate weapon: the power to say *Hey, we like you* or *Nope, sorry, you're not what we've got in mind.* They need exactly that authority to act right on the spot.

Remember this—your worst hire of every year is invariably the least likely to ever leave.

For non-college recruiting, this doesn't really change much other than the logistics. Your owners instinctively already know what you're looking for in the next owners. And the longer they've worked there, the more they'll quickly know exactly what you're not looking for. This is really important. It's not easy to know the difference between the malcontents who won't like anywhere they'll ever work (especially as hard as your employee owners work) and the ones who are truly looking for the unique opportunity that you have. Longtime employee owners, alongside very experienced and, with hope, longtime human resources recruiters, have the best chance to see it clearly.

And please don't rely solely on advertising job openings. For goodness sake, make your employee owners your primary recruiters. You can even avoid paying recruitment bonuses completely if you enlist your employee owners to use their networks to find the right people and make the pitch.

I can tell you people who are suited to ESOP culture are the ones who want to take charge of their own destiny.

—*Allen Xi, Senior Vice President, Burns & McDonnell (Houston office)*

Keep the Bus Tuned

At some point in this book, you may have decided to start a drinking game where you take a shot with each reference to Jim Collins or Joseph Blasi. Well, take your first one now and then hold onto something bolted down for this corollary: One bad employee equals the negative influence of ten great employees, according to Collins. And, according to Graves, double that with a bad owner.

Get the wrong employee owners off your bus.

> A warning to the boss: Inaction compounds the problems of the bad employee. Your employee owners know you know when it's time to get someone off the bus, and if you don't . . . well, you know what they're thinking now, don't you?

I'm not saying skip the necessary human resources processes, but *get them off and do it now*! One bad apple doesn't just spoil the whole bunch; its effect is viral and exponential when the employee is also an owner. The good news is, ESOPs attract and keep good employees—the "good eggs" I referred to in chapter two—but you'll have no problem identifying who needs to go because the rest of your employee owners will be religiously pointing them out.

> Job seekers are often just that: people looking for a job. You need owners.

Don't Grow Just to Grow—You're Not a Public Company!

I love watching CNBC, especially *Mad Money* with host Jim Cramer. He was my shining light throughout the COVID-19 economy, and he'd be happy to know that I kept the faith in American business. But you know what, I don't care much about CNBC's *Revenue Beats*. You can't pay bonuses with revenues, and you sure as heck won't create shareholder return with it either. Revenue beats help public companies—maybe—but they mean nothing to ESOPs. Don't grow just to grow.

In fact, when it comes to growing employment, I would recommend you be extremely picky. Job seekers are often just that: people looking for a job. You need owners. And recognizing the difference is anything but easy. They may not even know it themselves yet, especially if you're recruiting at American colleges.

Look for the Hunger—Don't Hire for Need, Hire for Want

Review the previous chapter on *WHO?* as necessary to remind you what you're looking for and learn quickly how to spot the right candidates. Your hiring goal is simple but not at all easy—pick the individuals you could imagine reacting to their shareholder reports in four to five years with a big "*Whoa!*" Soon enough, you're cutting cake at their retirement party—their "retired early" retirement party.

Retain What You've Gained: It All Adds Up to Zero

If employees aren't leaving, you're doing something right. I look at turnover goals as excluding retirements and terminations. One we should celebrate, and the other we should not. Beyond these two, 0 percent is the goal. Employee ownership with any kind of positive financial results will quickly get you most of the way home. It's that simple. It's not that easy, but it is that simple.

If employee owners are leaving, you're definitely doing something wrong. You should first be lasered in on one-year to three-year quitters. Occasionally, they just can't stand living far away from their parents or need to move back to the farm to help out poor old Uncle Pete. Those don't count. But if you're losing people within the first few years, it's time to take a hard look at what's really happening:

- **Are you being completely honest in recruiting?** ESOPs are a *great* place to work but not always an *easy* place to work. I cannot emphasize this enough. Employee owners will out-work your competition. They're not the go-home-early types. They're the ones who kept their grades up *and* were active in lots of extracurricular activities during their college years. You're looking for evidence of the axiom *how you do anything is how you do everything* in their lives. Learn to weed out the ones who can't engage and commit to the culture before you even hire them.

- **Are you starting ESOP training on day one?** You should be. Don't wait for their first annual statement, which may be too late. Go for some mini *whoas*! Recruiting the best employee owners doesn't end on their first day. Remember, you're creating believers, not followers. Early ESOP education should be geared accordingly. And make sure "their" boss or, even better, "the" boss teaches at least one of the training courses.

- **Are you targeting benefits to this specific workforce?** Some are bigger difference makers than others for newer employees, such as signing bonuses, on-site childcare, new mom nursing rooms, and so on. If you can throw in pet care, well, it worked great for Google! This is a tough one to hold back during recruiting but I love to have one benefit be a surprise to new employee owners until their first day of orientation.

Promote Your Owners

One of my favorite colleges in the world had one of the best department deans I've ever known. He wanted to be his university's provost and was excited to apply for the position when it opened. He not only didn't get the nod but was told that the university simply had to look outside because "it would make us all better." Based on that logic, he did the only thing he could. He applied elsewhere and not only won the provost position at an even bigger school but soon after became the president at one of America's largest universities (with a hell of a football team, too). The college I loved lost.

Promote-from-within is a solid management practice—no matter what and no matter where. But within the team-first culture of an employee-owned firm, this should be your standard operating procedure 99 percent of the time. Burns & Mac is again a perfect example, having had only one CEO in its history who wasn't promoted from within. And that was the founder (get it?).

There is just no way an outsider can understand your culture like you do. When you don't promote from within, you are way more likely to be disappointed in your decision and, worse, you just told everyone in the company that not a single person who works there was good enough. There are exceptions for sure, but even new executives often take years to fully understand the culture. So, at a minimum, when you are "forced" to look outside, remember what you're up against.

If you consistently need to look at outside candidates for key promotions, my advice to you is to take a good, hard look at your career and job transition planning practices. Every executive in your firm should have a minimum of three to four employee owners preparing to replace them. If you are successful at this clear-but-difficult management challenge, you will not only be well ahead of your competition, you'll be well ahead of even your ESOP challengers.

Promote on talent, nothing else.

> Promote-from-within is a solid management practice—no matter what and no matter where. But within the team-first culture of an employee-owned firm, this should be your standard operating procedure 99 percent of the time.

Another warning to the boss: Research by global management consultant McKinsey's Strategy and Corporate Finance Practice has long shown that CEOs making *bold moves* is vital to achieving outstanding performance, which itself is elusive—only one in twelve companies goes from being an average performer to a top-quintile performer over a ten-year period. Making one or two bold moves more than doubles the likelihood of making such a shift; making three or more makes it six times more likely.[5]

But troubling in the ESOP "promote-from-within" world, they also found that CEOs who are hired externally move with more boldness and speed than those hired within an organization, partly because of the social pressures that constrain internally promoted CEOs.[6]

ESOP CEOs, critically, cannot simply manage. They must lead, and they must do so boldly.

Rule 3: In Fast, Out Fast . . . but Not All at Once

Get Them In Fast!

You want that *Whoa* moment to come as fast as possible, and, as you might guess, so do your employee owners. One day they open their annual ESOP statement, and somehow, their ESOP valuation just exceeded their 401(k), or perhaps the value of their home, maybe even their annual salary. They weren't expecting it to happen so fast. For me, it was year five, but for many, it can be even sooner, especially if you are being aggressive with your ESOP cash allocation.

> When one of your employees gets to that *Whoa* moment, you just got yourself an employee owner for life. After *Whoa*, your turnover rates plummet, your risk-awareness soars, your client attentiveness reaches five-star, and so on.

When one of your employees gets to that *Whoa* moment, you just got yourself an employee owner for life. After *Whoa*, your turnover rates plummet, your risk-awareness soars, your client attentiveness reaches five-star, and so on. You want to reach that level as quickly as you can.

> I don't think the employees can see the big picture of the ESOP right away. It takes a while to see how much employee ownership can mean to you personally. It takes a couple of years to see how much stock you receive and the worth of the stock. I know I really had no idea what the outcome would be when we first became an ESOP.
>
> —Joel Iserman, associate (who saved Greg from the Armageddon)

Remember the *Why*: Owners work harder. Owners care more.

You want to get to *Whoa* just as fast as possible. That means you want new employees to earn stock just as fast as possible. *Don't use waiting periods!*

> Important Culture Point: Remember that your employee owners *earn* it. They don't *buy* it. And, they sure aren't *given* it. Technically, many use the word *grants*, but for me, it's *earned*. And when an employee gets to that *Whoa* moment, you just got yourself an employee owner for life.

Create your plan where new employee owners earn their first ESOP cash almost immediately and buy their first shares as soon as possible. Be certain that your individual ESOP reports are distributed to new employee owners quickly, perhaps even a special first-year report. Get them in fast! You want to get to *Whoa* just as fast as possible.

Get Them Out Fast!

It's almost as important to get your exiting employees *out fast*. We celebrated our retirees publicly at Burns & Mac . . . we celebrated mine . . . but when it's time to retire, it's time to sell.

You might be surprised how many ESOPs—great ESOPs—do five-year payouts. One of my all-time favorite ESOPs, Hy-Vee Supermarkets, has done exactly that in the past. Your former employee owners would absolutely love this policy, but it's not in the best interest of your long-term success. ESOPs that use payout periods have a good argument. It protects the firm in case of an economic turndown. The COVID-19 economy certainly backs up their point. Your ESOP should have structural safeguards (and a healthy rainy-day fund) to protect the firm, but don't let this risk determine your everyday policy. Make sure your plan allows for longer payouts in an emergency, but I don't recommend you make it a practice.

Do payouts to former employee owners, even retirees, as fast as possible.

You want to be 100 percent employee owned, and that just can't include retirees (like me). I admit I didn't go all in on this recommendation when I was the CEO of Burns & Mac. We allowed some employee owners based on tenure and age to cash out over two years. That was my mistake and was corrected by my successor, Ray Kowalik.

Love your employee owners but, again, get them *out fast*. Besides, with an almost immediate buyout (you guessed it) you are recycling those shares into the hands of newer employee owners faster.

But Not All at Once!

At Burns & Mac we paid down our original buyout loan in just eight years. From an economically conservative viewpoint, that sounds terrific. If I were the boss back then, I would have done exactly the same. But, if we started the ESOP again, I would pay off the initial loan at a more strategic pace. I don't consider this a huge difference maker, but it is a generational one.

Simply put, if you pay off the initial loan that fast you will overconcentrate your shares within one historical group of employees (I called ours "The Originals"), and it will take a generation before your distribution of shares normalizes. I think fifteen years would be a better span. If, over that time, your success blossoms as I would expect and you're wondering what to do with all that cash . . . well . . . see Rule 4.

Turning workers into owners will lead to explosive growth for your firm, so Rule 3 jumps in importance, also explosively. You want owners at the wheel of your firm. That means out with the old and in with the new as fast as possible.

Rule 4: Diversify Them . . . Diversify Them Hard

You read that header and you might just think I've lost it. Here I pound away at making everyone think like an owner, and now I want to diversify them? Yes, that's exactly correct.

Diversification solves a problem and has a great benefit, too.

Here's the dilemma: I've lost track of the number of times an outside financial advisor has recommended to one of our employee owners that their retirement savings, while fantastic, are too focused, and that they should just quit our place to protect their portfolio. To me, this amounts to punishing them for the success of their firm, and that's just insanity.

But, as much as I hate this, I understand why. Do you remember the Arthur Andersen story where one audit team doing just one bad (some say criminal) audit (of Enron) literally imploded a once terrific and über-successful firm? It's not an employee-ownership story, but it's a perfect example of how just one bad project, and a few bad apples, cost a lot of partners their lifetime fortunes. The Enron half of the story was also exacerbated by the fact that a lot of the employees' and partners' pain came from money taken out of weekly paychecks versus employee-ownership shares, which are earned grants.

Capitalism is not without risk. The few (very few) critics of employee ownership love this particular debate, especially those who believe most, if not all, American firms are operated by greedy, egocentric CEOs. We obviously run in different circles.

As the firm's fiduciary, however, this is the charge and challenge. And so, we want to take a lot of this risk, even if small, away from them. The solution? *Diversify them . . . diversify them hard.* Encouraging investment autonomy is not going to cost you—it's going to pay off. Here are some options:

401(k)

At first, having a 401(k) IRS Qualified Retirement Benefit might seem contrary to keeping everyone at maximum motivation to protect and grow the company, but for me this is a no-brainer. Overall, 401(k)s are terrific benefits. They motivate your employee owners to invest a portion of each paycheck that you match, and it diversifies them away from company stock. If it were me, I'd match at the 50 percent level, but this can be argued lower or higher.

There are some firms in America that still match their own firm's stock into 401(k) benefit programs. *Don't do it.* That is exactly not diversifying them away from your ESOP stock and reducing their risk. Fiduciary attorneys will likely recommend that you opt your employee owners into your 401(k) unless they specifically opt out. *Great decision.* They will also recommend that you encourage and/or limit your employees into target date-based retirement investments. *Brilliant decision.*

Dividend, Dividend, Dividend

If an American company, public or private, is making money, it should be paying out a portion of that directly to their shareholders in a dividend—it's that simple. I see American S&P giants all the time holding on to cash like they'll never make another nickel. Others, heroically, paid out consistently even during 2020. For ESOPs, it's an even easier decision. By taking money off your balance sheet and paying it out to the ESOP in dividends, you're not only managing your biggest long-term shareholder liability (by managing your stock price), you are diversifying their ESOP accounts away from your firm's ESOP stock. It's a double win.

Moreover, you're putting cash into all accounts more quickly, which helps ensure that your newer employee owners have enough cash in their accounts to purchase the maximum shares possible in their early years. Getting them to *Whoa!*

Here's a long-term goal: Recognizing that ESOPs are required to be "invested" primarily in company stock—50 percent of your most senior employee-owners' ESOP accounts should be in their cash balance. If you can get to that, even the hardest-selling financial advisor will have a tough sell to make.

It's not really in cash, of course. It will be invested by your ESOP committee into bonds/stocks and other investments. Not a lot of ESOPs have large cash accounts for their employee owners that are not only diversified but are invested with their ultimate retirement in mind . . . that's okay: You're not most ESOPs.

Dividends: Here's another great reason to maximize dividends, invest them, and grow your ESOP *cash*—it creates that rainy-day fund we discussed earlier for your ESOP. Whether times are good or bad, you're always going to have some employee owners leave your firm each year. When times are tough, perhaps due to recession or maybe just a couple of bad projects, this excess cash (in your employee-owners' ESOP accounts) gives you the tool you'll need to keep the ESOP flowing as you buy back shares with cash already in participant accounts. Further, excess cash in the ESOP gives you the flexibility to reduce ESOP cash contributions in down years. I would hate this as an executive but it beats taking on debt.

Let Senior Employee Owners Diversify Even More

Are you fifty or older? If you are, do you remember the first time you said to yourself, *I think I'm pretty well off for retirement, but I better make sure I have a plan?* And, given that great employee owners are financially responsible, motivated, and the "planner" type, this likely happens to most of them.

When your employees reach fifty, I would recommend that you encourage them (their decision here) to start diversifying out of your company ESOP stock. When they turn fifty-five, and then again at sixty, they should be allowed to diversify even more—maybe as much as 75 percent.

Here's what you'll likely find: Almost none will take you up on the offer. Your ESOP has likely worked out so well for them that they won't diversify at all. But it's very important that you make it available. Then do two things:

> If you insinuate that diversification is inherently a bad decision, or worse, some sort of loyalty test, you're risking their trust. *This is their call.*

- Make diversification an easy, educated option.
- Never, never, never recommend that they don't exercise it. If you insinuate that diversification is inherently a bad decision, or worse, some sort of loyalty test, you're risking their trust. *This is their call.*

Diversification rights give your employee owners the peace of mind that they're in control, which enables them to make their career choices logically. And if they do diversify, guess what—you just recirculated even more stock back to your newest employee owners.

Rule 5: Be Employee Owned, Not Employee Run

Here's what our nation's founders and the Constitution have in common with a well-run ESOP: When the Founding Fathers established America as a representative democracy—not an outright democratic state—it was with the advantages of strong, well-informed leadership in mind (make your own political joke here). Countries need strong leaders, and so do ESOPs. If every employee owner had to "vote" on every administrative decision on a daily basis, the work of the company wouldn't get done.

Just like a representative democracy, employee-owned firms need an efficient, effective, and informed process for leadership and decision making. The takeaway: Select the right leaders, and let them lead. If they fail, fire them and get new leadership.

There are only a couple of exceptions in my view—the most important one being the sale of the company. In that case, every employee owner should have a say. Other exceptions would be rarer, like liquidation and complete dissolution . . . here's hoping you never have to face any of that. When employee-owner votes are required, IRS Code, section 409(e), dictates how that occurs. Typically, each participant would vote according to their number of shares held in their ESOP accounts.[7]

> Just like a representative democracy, employee-owned firms need an efficient, effective, and informed process for leadership and decision making. The takeaway: Select the right leaders, and let them lead. If they fail, fire them and get new leadership.

So, no, we won't be voting on dress code, employee benefits, bonuses, and so on, but that doesn't mean we aren't going to take employee owners into a substantially higher level of engagement. There are many opportunities for the employee owners to directly influence policy and practice, including but not limited to:

- Charitable giving recommendations
- ESOP committees
- Employee representative committees
- Retirement asset investment committees
- Shareholder meetings
- Your best idea here

Indeed, the advantage of representative democracy applies to the leadership of any public company. Activist shareholders who try to run companies or influence their strategies almost always see short-term gains, because that's exactly how they think—short term. They are traders. CEOs should not act like traders. By the very nature of their title and function, they are duty-bound to think in the long-term interest of the firm and its shareholders.

The workers are the owners and your most important asset, but, in the end, you are the boss.

When I sent this section, "Be Employee Owned, Not Employee Run," to my critical review team, which was made up of some of the best academic minds and most successful firms in ESOP history, I got a lot of feedback. I heard everything from *Don't say that* to *You're about to ruin your whole premise.* And then I heard from others who responded to this section with *Bingo* and another who said, *Greg—this is exactly right!*

I worked at employee-owned Burns & McDonnell under a variety of leaders: an "academic," an "iron fist," and a "cheerleader" CEO. All achieved financial success. Not being run by the employee owners does not mean owners are not highly participative. In fact, ESOPs create the perfect opportunity for leaders with an engaged and participative approach to gain the maximum positive input from workers. Decisions made collaboratively can create maximum positive results. In the end, though, you are the boss. Your employee owners expect you to be the boss, and they expect you to be amazing at it.

Rule 6: Profit Is Not a Dirty Word

When employees are just employees, they are often ambivalent or even surly over how rich the boss is getting. They might even enjoy seeing the boss take one on the chin once in a while. Employee owners, on the other hand, will behave exactly the opposite if you'll just give them the chance. But they need to understand how an owner should think about the financial status of their ESOP. As my friend and former president of Burns & Mac's Construction/Design-

> The workers are the owners and your most important asset, but, in the end, you are the boss.

Build Group, Don Greenwood, used to say, "Profit is not a dirty word." You'll need to help employee owners gain the owner perspective.

Educate Them

Owners should know how profits are made at your company and how they are not. Owners should understand your financial statements, not just their annual ESOP statement. Owners should know the biggest drivers regarding profitability as well. No, the employee owners don't get to know how much their boss makes in compensation, but they do need to understand the interrelationships between:

- Compensation and performance
- Direct and allocated costs to profitability
- Overheads and net income
- And, eventually, share price

Early in my tenure as a Burns & Mac officer, I remember being surprised at how only a very few business statistics determined most of my monthly income statement. My thinking was off, and I had to quickly learn to identify the ones that really drove results. After I became CEO, when I would meet personally with groups of employees, I loved pulling out the list of operational overheads and challenging them to help me look for savings. It wasn't easy because 90 percent of our overheads were either support compensation (and we ran a very tight ship) or benefits paid directly to our employee owners. The overheads that people typically scream about don't usually amount to much. And if they understand what they're seeing on their monthly income statement, they scream even less.

> Educating your employee owners to comprehend their firm's income statement is a must.

This cannot be overstated: Educating your employee owners to comprehend their firm's income statement is a must. Start early with "ESOP 101" courses, but move on quickly to understanding complex financial statements. Just a few meetings will convince them as owners that profit is, indeed, not a dirty word.

Stress Confidentiality

Share, share, share information, but stress confidentiality? Let me explain. We had little to no trouble with this at Burns & Mac. We shared info like our employee owners were shareholders (because they are), but we stressed over and over again that this was no one else's business but our own. If an employee feels like an owner—because they are being treated like one— then that confidentiality is going to be upheld because that individual feels like he or she is on the "inside" of the circle of trust. *You have a big role here . . .* this requires transparency from executive leadership, and leaders who are worthy of that trust. They need to trust you first before you can trust them.

Prove It

If you're making doughnuts and you stress how important frosting efficiency is to the bottom line, and then if frosting efficiency doubles . . . well then, the employee owners of your doughnut shop had better see improved profits. They had better see a nice bonus this month, a better annual dividend, a higher stock price.

You will get exactly one strike on this. If you stress what it will take, you had better be right. If you're wrong, or worse, if you simply don't come through on promises, your employee owners will either think you have alternative goals or, worse, that you don't know what you're talking about.

Prove it to them . . . *show them the money.*

Be 100 Percent Honest

Have a big lawsuit facing the firm? Tell them. In fact, bring everybody inside on that . . . they'll find out anyway. Have a big, bad project that's going to cost everyone some of their bonus? Tell them. They might just jump in to help—like an owner. The financial statements you present to your employee owners are the same numbers the CFO presents to you and that your auditor and evaluation consultants see. There's no sugarcoating bad news, and no shading of good news either.

There are a few exceptions, beginning with confidential information from certain clients and, of course, with human resources issues. Yes, even employee-owned companies have occasional HR issues. People are people.

It's like my dad used to say, "Just be honest; then you won't have to remember what you said." The truth is always the truth. And, no, I'm not going to make another joke about presidential politics here (but I could).

Finally, Stress It: We Are a For-Profit Company

I used to include in every email I sent to employees what our billable percentages (what percent of our time is billable to a client project) were from the week before. Every week! *Why?* Not because every employee can impact it every week, but because billable time is important, *very* important, to our financial success, and I wanted our employee owners to know it. I wanted at least one message in every communication to my employee owners to be financial. It was never the only the message, of course, but it was never omitted.

Make sure that every time one of your employee owners get a bonus, they are told that bonuses start and finish with the firm's financial success. Even more, make sure that they know the quality and security of their retirement starts and finishes with the firm's financial profitability. They'll quickly learn that it's pretty much the only factor.

And here's a good one: Make sure that every employee owner knows that the company's philanthropy starts and finishes with the company's financial success. The profit we make helps us help others. *No Margin = No Mission.*

As Don Greenwood would say, *profit is not a dirty word.* Americans have understood this well from Jeffersonian times and on to today. Corporate success should not be defined as only financial—I hope that goes without saying. But it's very tough for American businesses to be more philanthropic, to be greener, to be more inclusive, and to achieve better compensation/retirement parity if they are not financially successful as well.

> Another warning to the boss: The more you stress it, the more they will expect it—short-term but, even more so, long-term financial success. Carver Edison found in its five-year study that public companies with employee ownership benefit plans averaged a 12 percent return on equity versus 7 percent for companies without the employee ownership advantage.[8] Remember *Who?* This is exactly the expectation of our people we were looking for. You expect it of them, and they expect it of you.

Rule 7: Communication Rules (Yes, Read That Both Ways)

Owners love to be communicated with . . . they want to know everything. Knowledge is power, and employee owners are an empowered people. They want to know when there's danger, but even more, they want to know when it's time to celebrate or maybe just to be proud. Communicate with them more often than you'd think would be necessary. In the tight balance between sharing necessary information versus wasting their time, let over-communication carry more of the weight.

Remember the words of the famous Irish playwright, critic, and political activist George Bernard Shaw: "The single biggest problem in communication is the illusion that it has taken place." Tell them what you're going to say; say it; then tell them what you said.

Again, this topic might seem obvious, but instead of thinking, *Here's something I already know,* understand that communication is one of your best opportunities to differentiate yourself as an ESOP firm. Here are some communication rules I recommend:

From The Boss

We've already established that ESOPs still need strong, effective leaders, and you're the boss. But in the accelerated leadership world, the employee owners must also have an absolute and complete faith in their leader for the ownership advantage to flourish. Hearing from you directly and often is a good tact. No, *Twitter is not talking to them directly,* but it's good to use all the platforms your employee owners are using to maximize the ways you are reaching them.

> Employee owners must also have an absolute and complete faith in their leader for the ownership advantage to flourish.

Send out a New Year's message with your hopes for the calendar year. If you are a mid-sized or larger firm, do it by video. Not all your employee owners know you that well. Let them get a visual on you.

Email them often with reports of good news, bad news, any news. I did this weekly, but monthly would still be excellent. Write it all or most of it yourself and in your words. No, don't just pop it in the company newsletter—they'll never believe you wrote it yourself.

Your employee owners want to know you, what makes you tick, what you like and hate. If you're comfortable, share some family stories. One week, I even reported what I had bought Deanna for our anniversary. Making it personal sends the message that you recognize everybody has a personal life, including you. You don't need to air your dirty laundry; in fact, *don't air your dirty laundry.* Just humanize and connect. It shows respect and compassion and relativity.

Employee owners want affirmation, inspiration, and the big picture. They want to know the plan—the Big Plan—for the future. *And they want to hear it directly from you.* Be accessible. Management-by-walking-around is an overused reference but an underutilized strategy. If you're like me, meetings will dominate your calendar if you let them. Instead, literally schedule yourself some walking-around time. Take your lunch in the cafeteria. Go to holiday parties where you're not the host. Take a meeting in their conference room or office instead of yours.

There is literally nothing more distracting from the corporate mission than workers not trusting the boss. Don't let someone else decide this for them. Directly communicate with them yourself. And just be you. Not your formal, stilted "annual report" voice but your voice . . . they'll love it.

From Their Boss

You might be The Boss, but you can't be everybody's individual boss. At companies across America, people often seem to love *The* Boss but not always *Their* Boss. In fact, a lot of studies indicate that *Their* Boss is the leading cause of employee turnover at professional services firms.

Inc. magazine studied over a decade of Gallup survey results and concluded that 50 percent of employees left their job "to get away from their manager to improve their overall life at some point in their career."[9] Gallup's CEO Jim Clifton summarized it up perfectly. "The single biggest decision you make in your job—bigger than all the rest—is who you name manager," according to Clifton. "When you name the wrong person manager, nothing fixes that bad decision. Not compensation, not benefits—nothing."[10]

Let's fix that. Managers should be judged first and foremost on the turnover rate of their best employees. They should be rewarded when it's terrific and suffer direct consequences when it's awful. Some people are incredibly smart and talented but still make awful bosses. Most firms correct this too slowly. *Don't be most.*

The Gallup results went further and recognized what traits people love most about their managers. No surprise—it starts with absolute honesty and trust. From there, workers look for managers who are supportive of them both personally and professionally and who give good recognition not only for results but for the raw talents they bring to their work. Finally, workers love managers who can and do display empathy.

Global training giant Development Dimensions International has assessed more than 15,000 leaders from more than 300 organizations and concluded that empathy—yes, empathy—rose to the top as the most critical driver of overall manager performance: specifically, the ability to listen and respond with empathy.[11]

Now, if you're going to hold them directly responsible, you must give these specific employee owners the power to be Their Boss. Too many firms give mid-level managers tremendous responsibility with little power to address HR issues. Again, another easy stumble. Terrific career planning tools and full ESOP management training are a great place to start.

As a Shareholder

Communicate with your employee owners directly as shareholders. Here are three strategies to get you started.

- Each shareholder should get a copy of an Annual Corporate Report. But in this case, I'll contradict what I told you earlier and not include confidential information. I would include limited financials, philanthropy, project news, big milestones, and so on. If you have marketing and communications professionals as good as my old team, you can pretty much set them loose on this. Pen a letter for it to your employee owners. *Write it yourself.*
- Your shareholders should be invited to a private, confidential, annual meeting. It should be telecast, if necessary, to as many locations as possible. I stress private and confidential—this is for current employee owners only. I was the CEO for thirteen years, and I have attended zero Burns & Mac annual meetings since retirement—exactly how it should be. The annual meeting can be pretty much whatever you'd

like it to be; I've tried all sorts of combinations. It absolutely should include confidential financial information. Don't short-play this. You are on display, so be absolutely certain of what you are presenting and be 100 percent rehearsed and ready.

You can include other members of leadership in the meetings, but just remember that employee owners want to hear from The Boss. If you do include others, consider using well-produced video instead of having too many folks live.

Oh, one more thing, make fun of yourself at least once.

- Your shareholders should get an individual Annual Shareholder Statement. If your employee owners are anything like mine, they're working too hard too often to pay enough attention to themselves. Be certain each employee owner does get the time and the attention to receive, review, and understand their Annual Shareholder Statement. In fact, this is a terrific opportunity for individual, empathic communication from *Their* Boss.

  Remember: We're going for *Whoa!* Don't assume every employee owner knows how your ESOP works and how to read this statement—easy and comprehensive is the goal. Provide a link or phone number where they can get more help if they need it.

Rule 8: Implement Performance-Based Pay (and Why I Love, Love, Love It)

I remember a Major League Baseball manager saying once that if he could only have an entire team of players in the last year of their contracts, he'd win the World Series every year. Why? It's performance-based pay.

Again, you might think that the motivation of a wonderful and economically stress-free retirement should serve as more than enough motivation. You'd be right. But let's add some steroids to the mix and find the explosive results we're looking for—that's performance-based pay.

Bigger raises for high performance aren't enough. Better promotional opportunities aren't enough. And, as much as I hate to admit it, great communications all across your firm are not enough. Sorry, but nothing motivates high achievers more than the end-of-year scorecard that is performance-based pay.

I love spot bonuses; they have their place, especially if they are public in nature and fun, but they mean nothing compared to an annual, solid, universal, well-defined, and defendable year-end bonus program of performance-based pay. *Let's get this right.*

> Let's add some steroids to the mix and find the explosive results we're looking for—that's performance-based pay.

The characteristics of the best performance-based pay programs are:

- **Annual**: This might seem obvious but it's not. Employee owners must understand that performance-based pay is thanks to this year's firm-wide results *and* their contribution to it. Results vary at all firms, as does individual performance. This year's bonus guarantees nothing for future years. I had an old boss who liked to say (actually, in a very positive way) that on every January 1, all our bonuses were back to zero.
- **Solid**: Year-end bonuses must be meaningful. A truck full of frozen Christmas turkeys will not get this done. In fact, the higher the possibility, the better. I would even rather risk losing a few people over below-average base pay than not leave enough room in my plan for some mega-performance bonuses for my highest achievers.
- **Universal**: If the CEO gets a bonus, everybody gets a bonus. There may be a rare occasion when an employee owner doesn't get a bonus but that is typically a one-off performance issue. I've personally given out thousands of year-end bonuses over the years, and most of my all-time favorites were the small surprises that ended in tears. It is important that this is recognized throughout. The CEO might get the biggest bonus but they are also the first to take a hit.
- **Well Defined**: Employee owners should know what is expected of them and have at least some frame of reference for their bonus potential. But don't take this one too far. You don't want your employee

owners spending their days calculating their bonuses throughout the year. In fact, that makes it impossible to ever surprise them to the high side.

- **Defendable**: Very important. If an employee owner is surprised by his or her bonus, *I hope it's because it's high.* If they are surprised that it is low, The Boss or *Their* Boss hasn't communicated with them properly all year. It's perfectly okay for employee owners to get lower bonuses when the firm has a tough year. It is likely to have happened to 90 percent of CEOs in 2020. As long as that's well understood, it actually substantiates that your performance-based pay program is always working on behalf of the shareholder.

For this particular *How*, I don't need anybody's research or opinion to know this is exactly what your firm should be doing. But . . . it's always nice to have a wingman, and the research from Dr. Blasi and team shows it clearly again: "Our research shows that employee share ownership works best when combined with short-term profit sharing or gain sharing, a supportive corporate culture that provides the opportunity for employee involvement in solving company problems, training, job security, and, very important, a fair market-level wage for the employee's position and region. If a company thinks it can cut an employee's pay by 5 to 10 percent or more and then say, 'Oh, you can make it up in stock,' this company will fail with employee share ownership."[12]

> You want to win the World Series? Institute annual, solid, universal, well-defined, and defendable performance-based pay.

You want to win the World Series? Institute annual, solid, universal, well-defined, and defendable performance-based pay.

Rule 9: Get Your Oversight Right

In chapter three I promised we'd talk about bringing in the fiduciaries. Let's start with the CEO. Technically—legally—you are not necessarily a fiduciary in this role. But to me, being the CEO of an employee-owned company makes you just about the perfect example of what the word *fiduciary* means. In any event, getting this right is very important and you should not go it alone. Start by hiring an experienced ESOP ERISA attorney. Ours—Bob Grossman with Kansas City–based Polsinelli law firm—was terrific.

Fiduciary responsibilities also extend to your board of directors, ESOP trustee(s), and your ESOP committee, as I pointed out in the chapter on *What*. There is no one right way or wrong way (okay, there probably are some wrong ways) to fulfill those obligations, but here's my advice:

Convene an ESOP Committee for One and Only One Purpose

There is a reason some people call their ESOP committee their ESOP *Fiduciary* Committee: It is the ultimate boss. Its purpose is to elect the firm's board of directors; its duties range from making decisions about plan assets to assuring your ESOP complies with ERISA. Ultimately, the ESOP committee's biggest responsibility comes down to this one action: to vote the shares of the ESOP when necessary (which isn't very often for public or private companies).

ESOP committee votes might appear to be simple formalities. They are not. If your ESOP committee meets annually, they should be reminded by the committee's chair and probably by your general counsel of its singular duty to act on behalf of the shareholder in this moment.

I've said this already but it's worth repeating: The ESOP committee should not be allowed to vote the ESOP shares in the unfortunate event of the firm being for sale. That vote should push down to the employee owners with advice from the company's board and the ESOP trustee.

Start a Second ESOP Committee

Start another ESOP committee, and I don't really care what you call it. I like "ESOP Administrative Committee," but there are few wrong answers. I would include some board members, but I would also include a number of employee owners who are at least vested (even better, vested ten years or more).

This group would have a ton of less scary but still fiduciary duties including, for example, the administration of share turnover and how ESOP cash accounts are invested. Give them even more responsibilities if they're up to it. They will need strong HR support.

This group should meet much more often, quarterly at the minimum. Because they are making investment decisions, they should have a wholly independent financial advisor who should be excluded from investment opportunities to maintain absolute independence.

Build Your Board: Big/Small, Insiders/Outsiders, and Diversity

It's best practice for a board of directors to be made up of both insiders and independents. It is equally unquestioned that a board with a diversity of thought and life experience is better than a board that all looks alike.

Corporate boards in America, in fact, are trending more and more diverse and more and more independent. I don't agree with one growing trend, though, that board chairs must also be independent of the CEO. There are a lot of CEOs who wouldn't make great board chairs, but there are just as many who can be terrific in both roles. Don't default to the independent chair when your CEO can perform both roles more efficiently.

Great board makeup is easy to say, but tougher to build. Let's break it down.

- **Numbers:** Employee-owned firms should have small boards. This is not your local not-for-profit. You don't need thirty-three board members to help you fundraise all across town and all over the country. This is also not a public company subject to the usual "eleven or smaller" thought. I would recommend you try to keep your board to seven or less. You'll be nimbler, it will cost you less, and, if you choose wisely, there's still plenty of room for independent thought and valued diversity.
- **Composition:** The reason shareholders of public companies demand that the vast majority of board members be independent is to make certain that the board is the CEO's boss (and not the other way around). It makes the fiduciary roles very clear. At ESOPs, many examples of

predominantly independent-member boards, however, resulted from companies that got themselves into fiscal problems. If you believe—and I mean 100 percent believe—that your insider board will behave independently when they are inside the boardroom (mine certainly did), you do not need outsiders—technically. *It's a risk, and not a small one.*

For nearly all of you, having one or two independent board members is a good idea. Pay them well, require 100 percent attendance, and accept nothing less than full voice of them.

- **Recruitment**: Finding the right board members is critical, but let's first remember an important fact: CEOs don't pick boards . . . but boards do pick CEOs. It is the job of the entire company board to evaluate future members. Choosing between insiders can be tricky, as these are often "once in a career" moments for candidates. The most deserving might not be the talent area your current board needs, and vice versa. Take your time. These are big decisions. During interviews, I would always ask:

  ○ If I, as CEO, deserved it, could you vote to fire me?
  ○ When the boardroom door is closed, do you promise that you will fight like hell for what you believe?
  ○ When the door opens, will you fight like hell for what the group has decided?

  If you're looking for independents, my first recommendation for you is not to interview former employee owners—including and especially your former CEO. Your current CEO needs to be challenged by the board, but not second-guessed. I would start by seeking out an absolute expert in Employee Stock Ownership Plans—probably an American ESOP CFO or CEO from another firm. There are many to choose from. If you're looking for two, think back to our discussion on accelerated leadership in the post–COVID-19 world. Interview the best leaders you can find who will challenge you constantly to be better.

- **Diversity**: Boards are best when they have a diversity of thought. In America, that requires a diversity of life experiences. Quit thinking, please, that this is something to do because you're "required" or because the world is watching. No, absolutely, no. You do this because *it will make your board better, often significantly.* I was elected by a board of four white men; I left behind a board of six white men. I failed at this. During my thirteen years as CEO, I'm proud of creating a position for a Diversity Advocate, and the hiring of Michelle Word.

  I also promoted our first female C-level executive—a complete star and our first African American Regional Office Manager.

  > Boards are best when they have a diversity of thought. In America, that requires a diversity of life experiences.

  I have more examples, but they are just me playing defense. I fully admit I ran out of time to elect our first member who would bring greater diversity to our board of directors. This is a mistake you can avoid entirely, so plan accordingly and include diversity—no excuses.

  > The world is different than it was when the company was started in 1898. Decision makers are different, and the reasons that decisions are made are different. Greg wanted to better acclimate to the times. He understood why people felt marginalized and envisioned that we could do a better job being equitable.
  >
  > —Michelle Word, Burns & McDonnell Diversity Advocate

- **Voting**: If you need to have roll-call votes with your board, you have a very big problem. Decisions should always be made with consensus, then votes will be non-issues.

  Finally, no, 100 percent *no*: The employee owners do not get to vote on the board. There are some firms where this has actually been done successfully, but they are a rare breed. I would avoid this annual distraction from your mission.

Hire the Right ESOP Trustee

There are various views on this topic, but mine is that you clearly must hire an ESOP trustee—one with proven expertise in ESOPs. After all, the single most important ESOP moment of every year occurs the day your trustee and the share price valuation consultant recommend the new annual share price to your board.

The valuation consultant and trustee must be fiercely independent. Technically, they may only "*recommend*" the annual share price, but only a board of idiots wouldn't accept it. I would want at least some control over this process and the only way to do that is to hire a "directed trustee."

The term "directed trustee" came from ERISA (Employee Retirement Income Security Act of 1974). By definition, a directed trustee is there to assist in the administration of private retirement plans that are under the governance of ERISA.

Let's be clear: Being "directed" does not excuse your ESOP trustee from all fiduciary roles and responsibilities. It certainly doesn't mean that the valuation consultant loses independence or importance. But (a very big *but* here), it does put the duty and the risk squarely back on the firm's board of directors and perhaps on your ESOP committee.

In essence, nearly all believe you have this risk anyway. I'd want to be in control. My strong recommendation is that you hire your own directed ESOP trustee. Don't go cheap, don't delegate; be involved in this decision. If you have as good a Chief Financial Officer as I did, this is a team game between the two of you, but then a board decision.

Hire a Specialized Record Keeper

COVID-19 happens. A global recession happens. And now your board tells you it's time to cut costs. Bringing record keeping for your ESOP accounts in-house seems like an easy place to start. *Stop.* This isn't easy if you view it the way I do.

Your record keeper is more of a partner than you might think. Your shareholders like to know how their accounts are doing (just like public company shareholders). You may even want real-time reporting. You clearly want accounts to be highly accurate. And I hope you want high value, high service, and super low fees.

The answer is—you want all of these. For a 500-person ESOP, record keeping shouldn't cost you more than about $15,000 annually. The costs are paid for by the company (and not out of ESOP accounts) 99 percent of the time, and that's exactly what I would recommend.

The takeaway: There are partner firms that will do all this for you. You need their specialization. Bring in a third-party record keeper—you won't regret it.

Hire Your Other Boss

The toughest boss I ever had (despite my earlier reference to the bulldog) was actually Steve Gross, our executive compensation consultant with Mercer's Global Executive Compensation Group. He never yelled, rarely argued, and always wanted me to be successful. But let there be no doubt, he was the toughest. Every year he would ask me the toughest questions that I wasn't always ready to face. If our board and I didn't perform—on safety, on shareholder return, on succession planning—we didn't get paid. There were no excuses.

> As a tightly held, private, employee-owned firm, you should want the most qualified, most thorough, and toughest executive compensation consultant possible.

That's exactly what you should be looking for: high expectations, toughness, and integrity. As a tightly held, private, employee-owned firm, you should want the most qualified, most thorough, and toughest executive compensation consultant possible. It's also okay, by the way, if they believe in performance-based pay as much as I do. You should be pleading with them for the lowest base pay possible and the highest incentive program in your market.

This is a big deal—this is the person who's going to design your compensation plans with the goal of creating and evaluating the proper incentives for employee behavior. The compensation consultant should have multiple ways to evaluate performance, but only one of those should dominate the conversation after safety: What was your firm's return on investment to its employee-owner shareholders last year?

$$\frac{\text{DELTA IN SHARE PRICE} + \text{DIVIDENDS}}{\text{LAST YEAR'S SHARE PRICE}} = \text{ROI}$$

IF ROI = 20%

YOU GET TO CALL YOUR
PERSONAL INVESTMENT
ADVISOR WITH GOOD NEWS.

IF ROI = 5%

YOU GET TO KEEP YOUR JOB...
FOR NOW.

Here's the Rub

If the ESOP committee votes the shares, then they elect the board.

The board . . .

- Approves the pay of and hires (and fires) the CEO
- Hires and monitors the performance of the ESOP trustee and the compensation consultant
- Approves share price
- Nominates future board members

And just to come full circle, the board appoints the ESOP committee. Mark me: Circularity = Risk. *That's why ESOPs must get their oversight right.*

Rule 10: Be *the* Best Place to Work

If I have a personal hero even beyond Jim Collins (take another shot), it's the late Henry Bloch, the founder and CEO of H&R Block. Talk about your member of the Greatest Generation: Henry Bloch was a WWII navigator, defeated tyranny, went on to become one of Kansas City's most successful entrepreneurs, and left behind one of the most philanthropic families I have ever known. Just a few weeks after I became the CEO of

Burns & McDonnell in 2004, Henry invited me to lunch. He told me he'd been "thinking about my company" . . . I was about to find out what that meant.

I knew it was going to be a thrill to meet one of my town's most important citizens, but then halfway through my chicken sandwich, I had taken so many notes I had to ask our waiter Stevie for extra paper. As we were almost finished, Henry said, "So you guys are owned by your employees, right?" I said yes and pumped up my chest a bit. He asked, "So why aren't you a better place to work?"

Hmm. I was really taken aback. I said I thought we were a pretty good place to work and offered a few examples, including the ESOP. He gave what many would recognize as his patented headshake and said, "Not good enough, Greg, not good enough." He was right.

I had a lot of work to do.

It's just silly, if not lazy, not to do whatever this takes, right? If you own the place, why would you not want your firm to be one of the best places to work in America? And, if everybody owns the place, this elevates the goal to an absolute duty of leadership.

In 2004, as the new CEO, I took Henry's advice to heart, and, along with information, intuition, and inspiration, we worked harder than ever to be *great* for our people . . . our owners. It really comes down to this: It doesn't matter what your business is; just be the kind of place employees want to work at and never leave.

Regardless of the Product

After anything Jim Collins has written (down the hatch), my second favorite management book is *Fish!*[13] It describes the management philosophy in place at the Seattle Fish Market. Their product is fish. They sell fish, for goodness' sake, and still have managed to be one of the Best Places to Work in America. They also throw fish—to each other, to their customers, and to anybody else they might see walking by. How in the heck could that place become a great place to work? But that is exactly what they've done with the help of one of my most important management principles . . . be present.

Greg with his hero Henry Bloch (left) as Bloch awards Greg the
Henry Bloch award for promoting justice (2015)

Being a great place to work isn't about the product; it's a leadership
decision that *we will make this happen.*

Be Present

My favorite *Fish!* principle is, indeed, to *Be Present*. Many of us need to practice this. With so many demands on our time, we often put "being present"
way down on the list of priorities. When
was the last time you were completely there
in someone else's moment? This principle
means you are focused, listening, and even
empathizing with someone—not checking
your phone or making coffee at the same
time. Do you have the ability to under-

> Easy is not Great. Easy is Lazy.
> *Great is Hard.*

stand the private world of another person as if it were your own? Are you just
going through the motions or are you genuinely present at work?

I don't care what your product is. Read the list of *Fortune* magazine's 100 Best Companies to Work For in America from any year. You'll find every possible product—everything from grocery stores to travel consultants to engineering firms (I like that one a lot) to healthcare providers and, yes, to fish markets.

What they've all got in common *is a value and the ability for being present* right now in real time to their customers . . . and to each other.

Even If It's Not Easy

I say great, not easy. At Burns & Mac, we work on the world's hardest challenges; we work extremely hard at them, we travel a ton, and we are sometimes even a bit too demanding of each other. And yet, *Fortune* has named Burns & Mac one of America's 100 Best Companies to Work For ten times as of this writing.

Easy is not Great. Easy is Lazy. *Great is Hard.*

Sometimes You Do Just Need to Show Them the Money

You can be doing everything right, but if your employee owners believe the pay is unfair, biased, or preferential, it just won't matter. When the company has a great year—*you had better show them the money.* This is true on both an individual basis and an overall basis.

This also means that to pay a mega-bonus to that project manager who just broke all the profit records, you're going to have to pay someone else less. Maybe a lot less. Fair is fair even when it's bad.

> There is a friendly competition . . . we'll joke with one another, but we understand. "Every dog has his day" but, ultimately, we want all divisions to see success. While some receive larger incentives based on performance, we are really diversified, so we all ride the wave higher together.
>
> —*Gabe Hernandez, Vice President,*
> *Transmission & Distribution Services, Burns & McDonnell*

Because Happiness Is a Benefit

Being employee owned is a terrific start, but it's not enough. The ESOP is the world's best retirement program, but it does not, in and of itself, make your company a great place to work. It does, however, by its very definition, give you at least a couple of good steps forward.

First, I'll repeat this: It's the world's best retirement program. That alone will ensure longer-tenured employee owners. *And longer-tenured almost always means happier.* You'll prove this to yourself over time when you begin the employee surveys we're about to discuss.

Second, ESOPs provide lots of opportunity to communicate with your employee owners more often. Unless you're really bad at this, more communication from the top always produces happier workers. As we discussed earlier, the most important thing here is that the boss does this personally. Communication from the top cannot be delegated.

Employee owners are happier workers.

Not to Mention Some Other Benefits

Benefits alone won't get you the call from *Fortune* magazine or even your local business journal, but there are a few perks that can move this particular needle. They aren't the typical ones because your employee owners already expect solid healthcare insurance, paid holidays, and, at minimum, three to five weeks off for personal time, among others.

The benefits that move the best-place-to-work needle have to make a difference (and are perceived to make a difference) to career advancement and/or work-life balance. Solid, long-term, and absolutely honest career plans are a great way to start, teamed with 100 percent reimbursable higher education and training benefits.

Career-planning meetings are particularly important within the employee-ownership model. Workers at employee-owned firms who become believers quickly want to be difference makers—both to the firm and to their fellow employee owners. That, in itself, makes them both keenly interested in their own careers *and* interested in whether or not *Their Boss* empathizes with their ambitions.

Career-planning meetings at ESOPS are:

- Annual
- One-on-ones with *Their Boss*
- Not part of the annual performance review
- Not part of compensation discussions
- Not rushed, not spontaneous
- Never canceled

The work/life balance benefit ideas can go on forever. In addition to those I've already mentioned, how about offering:

- On-site oil changes and car detailing
- Dry cleaning pickup and delivery
- On-site healthcare
- Early childhood education
- On-site pharmacy
- An affordable (or free) healthy cafeteria
- On-site workout facilities
- A place for new moms to take nursing or pumping breaks

Get creative. It's simply amazing how many of these personal services companies will come to you if you just ask.

Just remember, *you're not trying to make it an easier place to work, just the very best one possible.*

Empowerment Is Everything

At America's very best places to work, employees are empowered to make decisions that are appropriate for their role, at a minimum. And you're the leader who has to imbue them with that capacity. Trust them to act accordingly, knowing full well that there will be mistakes made along the way to mastery. Let the mistakes happen because that's how we climb the learning curve. There is nothing that defeats an employee owner's attitude at work more than having his or her decisions overruled by a supervisor again and again. It's exactly how not to encourage the autonomy you're seeking from your people. If you want them to act like owners, well then, you'll need to let them do exactly that.

Think how annoying it is when you're on the phone forever with some firm's "service agent" only to be told, eventually, that a manager will have to be enlisted to resolve your issue. It can make you downright angry. But the only person more frustrated than you is that poor rep who hasn't been given the training or support or, most likely, the authority to make you happy.

In an ESOP culture, *employees are innately empowered by their ownership of the company.* Competently empowered employee owners create happy customers. And, that's one more step toward *Fortune* magazine calling you with good news.

> Competently empowered employee owners create happy customers. And, that's one more step toward *Fortune* magazine calling you with good news.

> The clients begin to realize they're working with owners, and promises that get made are promises kept.
>
> —*Darrell Hosler, former Executive Vice President, Burns & McDonnell*

In the Interests of Fairness

Okay, I promised myself when I started this chapter that I would not use the *culture* word even once, but I'm about to use it again. It may be overused in business, but it's the unavoidably right word in this context. An ESOP culture begins with demonstratable and recognizable fairness. If your people sense that office politics matter more than results, your firm is not the Best Company to Work For, or even in the running. Worse, if employee owners believe that gender, age, race, religion, or sexual orientation make any difference to *The Boss* or *Their Boss*, forget about this chapter and think about hiring a good human resources law firm instead.

> An ESOP culture begins with demonstratable and recognizable fairness.

Fairness culture is about more than just the legal angles. It can be demonstrated by you in so many ways, but the clearest is to lead by example. Your employees share ownership of this company with you—*treat them like you want to be treated.*

It's Okay to Be Proud of Where You Work

The guys at the Seattle Fish Market have fun at work, but that's not the most important message of *Fish!*. They believe that their place of business is important, and they believe they are very good at it. They are proud of where they work.

Making your company a place where employees are proud to work is your job, if you're the CEO, *and* if you're an owner. It's not marketing's job. It's not public relation's job either, although they'll play their part if you've done your part right. As CEO, my part in this was to remind, affirm, and proclaim our firm was really good at doing important work that changed the world in a positive way: groceries, healthcare, engineering, manufacturing—all yes.

> As CEO, my part in this was to remind, affirm, and proclaim our firm was really good at doing important work that changed the world in a positive way.

Creating a great place to work is all yours—and mine and ours. This is a huge ESOP advantage because pride of ownership is instinctive. In an ESOP, it's both individually and collectively motivating and validating. *Employees who are also owners take greater pride in their product and their place of work.*

Say It, Say It, Say It

In and of itself, being employee owned gives you the right to start calling yourself a Best Place to Work. Even if you've not made the *Fortune* magazine list yet, I sincerely believe it's crucial to identify yourself as such, and to actually *say* it. Certainly, you have to be somewhat careful not to come across as insincere, patronizing, or just like a big dummy, but I can't stress this enough. Say it, say it, say it . . . all the time: *We are a Great Place to Work.*

Part of ensuring your company is a Best Place to Work is setting expectations for everyone around you. From your most senior executives to the new employee owner on her first day, affirming this goal out loud and clearly shows what's important to you and that you won't settle for or tolerate anything else.

Now Prove It

Here we go, time to prove you mean it. *Publicly.*

Start immediately. Let your employee owners know that this *is* going to happen and that you need their input to become the Best Place to Work. Ask everyone everything: What do you need to do your job better? How can we solve a long-standing problem together? Where should we be headed next as a firm? Don't short-play this. This isn't just you walking around the office for a few hours. You will need to do full-scale employee satisfaction surveys to document all that input.

If the company is headed in the wrong direction, be honest—with yourself, for starters. Publish the results as much as possible, while protecting confidentiality when applicable. Announce at least one immediate change based on those results. It doesn't have to be something completely over the top like taking the whole firm to the Bahamas for a free vacation (as one of *Fortune*'s top companies did a few years back), but it does need to make your employee owners realize the Best Place to Work thing is going to happen and soon.

Now immediately begin applying for recognition. Don't wait. Apply every year to every possible source that makes these commendations. *Fortune*'s list is, of course, the most famous, but there are only about 100 other Best Places to Work programs out there. One of my favorites was our local business journal. Find them online and start applying now. Apply locally and nationally. Again, publish the findings as much as possible and let everyone see the improvements.

And when you win (and you are going to win), it's *party time*.

I don't care if you're only named the 100th Best Place to Work on your block—celebrate the absolute hell out of it.

I remember the first time Burns & Mac made the *Fortune* list (we were number 50). Melissa Wood and I emailed the employee owners in our Kansas City office (and regional office managers did the same across the country) with the great news, and I told them to meet me in the front parking lot in five minutes. By the time I left my office, I was almost trampled by hundreds of employee owners in the stairwells. As we all headed to the first floor, three semi-trucks full of Kansas City's finest micro-brewed beer pulled up. As my officers and I passed out about 2,000 six-packs, I remember one employee owner telling me, "Well, Greg, if we aren't the Best Place to Work already, we will be by five o'clock!"

> I don't care if you're only named the 100th Best Place to Work on your block—celebrate the absolute hell out of it.

Say it now to yourself before reading further: "*I will make my firm* the *Best Place to Work*."

Fortune names Burns & McDonnell as 50th best place to work in America, 2009

How?

That was a whole lot of *How!* I hope it gives you a solid start on your own
ESOP. If I could boil it down to one guiding principle as to *how* you implement your ESOP, it would be this: Your employees are the owners; you
want them to act like owners; and so, you should treat them like owners.

Your Employees Are the Owners, So Treat Them Like Owners

Go 100 Percent
Hire and Promote "Owners"
Get Them In and Out Fast
Diversify Them . . . Diversify Them Hard
Be Employee Owned, Not Employee Run
Profit Is Not a Dirty Word
Communicate!
Implement Performance-Based Pay
Bring in the Fiduciaries
Be One of America's Best Places to Work

CHAPTER 6

Only in America

You Can Own Your Own Future

There is something uniquely American about individual ownership. It's in the DNA of our country to inspire a vastly colorful although often stubborn melting pot of people both individually and collectively with this singular, extraordinary truth: You can own your own future.

When Pulitzer Prize–winning historian James Truslow Adams wrote, "Life should be better and richer and fuller for everyone, with opportunity for each according to ability or achievement," in 1931, he was trying to define the American Dream.[1] He could have just as easily been describing the potential of each and every American employee owner.

The theories on employee ownership and economic justice are certainly not germane only to America or Americans. But, as with so many things in this nation's history, we are in a unique position to capture these advantages in a greater and more profound way. It is the advantage of a nation that was born of genius, conceived in liberty, and dedicated to the pursuit of happiness. So now, before we conclude, let's take a look at how some of history's greatest communicators viewed the American experience and explore how those views dovetail with the empowering idea of employee ownership.

From Our Very Beginning

The Revolutionaries did not intend to provide men with property so that they might flee from public responsibility . . . property was, rather, the necessary basis for a committed republican citizenry.[2]
—Drew R. McCoy, historian

The founders of our country *trusted* that if early Americans were autonomous owners of their property and completely self-reliant for survival, this grand experiment called America would not only be a success for liberty, but for personal and joint economic prosperity as well. Historian Drew McCoy articulated this perfectly when he wrote, "The personal independence that resulted from the ownership of land permitted a citizen to participate responsibly in the political process, public good, rather than the narrow interest of the men—or government—on whom he depended for support."[3]

Read both McCoy quotes again, please. Do you cringe? I did. Our founders intended that the "fortunate" should become servants of this nation . . . and not just through philanthropy. How many "servant leaders" do you know who would make incredible mayors, legislators, or maybe even more, but who are so turned off by the politics of the twenty-first century that they simply won't put themselves or their families through the meat grinder? McCoy's words argue: *The nation is calling on you still.*

Instead, today in Washington, D.C., I too often see McCoy's "narrow interest" and "dependency" dominating the debate.

Owners working harder than their non-owner competitors will not only achieve the personal success they earn and the economic justice they deserve, they will deliver a more robust economy for the nation as a whole.

His cautionary insight was already red-alarming a lot of early twenty-first-century, self-interested corporate behavior. The need for statesmanship will become exponentially more critical in the post-pandemic world. We have got to reset our course to its originating values.

Along with personal liberty, the right of personal ownership is, arguably, the great breakthrough and legacy of our founders' brilliant vision. Owners working harder than their non-owner competitors will not only achieve the personal success they earn and the economic justice they deserve, they will deliver a more robust economy for the nation as a whole.

Right Here . . . Right Now

America is too great for small dreams.
—President Ronald Reagan

President Reagan was one of the greatest communicators of our time. Not everyone loved everything he believed (I almost always did), but it was hard to deny his most famous expressions:

"Mr. Gorbachev, tear down this wall."

"I believe the best social program is a job."

"It has been said that politics is the second-oldest profession. I have learned that it bears a striking resemblance to the first."

But none of those is my personal favorite. In 1985, President Reagan formed a Presidential Task Force called *Project Economic Justice.* Its 1986 report, *High Road to Economic Justice,* was America's first official endorsement of "expanded capital ownership" as a means for achieving economic democracy as the foundation for sustaining a stable political order.

Some of the task force's recommendations were adopted into U.S. foreign policy and were included as one of the World Bank's "market-based" options for debt-equity conversions through Employee Stock Ownership Plans (ESOPs).[4]

In 1987, President Reagan declared: "I can't help but believe that in the future we'll see in the United States and throughout the Western world an increasing trend toward the next logical step—Employee Ownership."[5]

Good news. More than thirty years later, there has never been a better place or a better time for ESOP possibilities than now. American entrepreneurism has never been at a higher pitch. Despite a tough 2020, inherent demand within the American economy has work for your firm—lots and lots of work. There is technical and fiduciary help for you everywhere, and the American federal tax system is cheering for you to say yes.

Employee ownership is in the sweet spot for tens of millions of American workers who have a bent toward ownership even if they aren't enormous risk-takers ready to start at zero. Let's face it, even Clinton S. Burns and Robert E. McDonnell had side jobs at first.

Despite what the far right *and* the far left might want you to believe, the American worker will still out-*think*, out-*work*, and out-*care* their foreign counterparts *if* they are given the chance for economic justice as an owner. Washington and Jefferson were right 250 years ago, President Reagan was right in 1987, and they're still right now.

Without Apologies

> I believe in striving for excellence. I sweat the big and small stuff! I do not apologize for this.[6]
> —Dr. Anthony Fauci

In 2020, who would have guessed that a seventy-nine-year-old physician from Brooklyn, New York, would become one of the world's most recognized, important, and influential leaders? While a small minority criticized Dr. Anthony Fauci's unflinching, conservative advice, most of us listened—*intently*. In the past, he'd worked tirelessly on curing diseases like HIV/AIDS, but until the novel coronavirus pandemic, Dr. Fauci wasn't widely known outside certain circles. Then he became the much-needed voice of science during the COVID-19 medical crisis.

Similarly, America now desperately needs to "sweat the big and the small stuff" to find the real solutions for full economic recovery.

Future pandemic responses (with hope, far into the future) will be in the hands of the leaders of this nation with help, I pray, from the experts at the NIH and CDC. But the future of American prosperity needs two important additional cures that lie at the feet of our business leaders: one for our economy and one for economic disparity.

Don't get me wrong: We are going to recover the post-pandemic economy and compete like crazy, thanks to the will of the American worker. But let's give these efforts another dose of steroids by making employee owners of at least another fourteen million American workers—that'd be twice the current count. And it'd be a quantum leap in the right direction.

If we do that, the strength of the American economy would also improve exponentially. How much? Good question. Remember this all-important *Why*: Employee-owned firms are more productive, will grow faster, and will outcompete their foreign competitors. That's a given to me and supported by the research as well.

> We are going to recover the post-pandemic economy and compete like crazy, thanks to the will of the American worker. But let's give these efforts another dose of steroids by making employee owners of at least another fourteen million American workers.

Improving American economic competitiveness while simultaneously resolving wealth disparity is not a simple puzzle. China, India, and other nations became economic powerhouses in the last century but unconscionably increased their number of poor households in the process. Indeed, their approach put billions of children into what many would argue is nothing more than servitude.

In spite of the financial urgency we face, I have more faith in the American worker than in a technology-driven, capital-intensive hive mind driving our economic recovery. Without conscious intervention, commerce at all costs will only increase wealth disparity in the long run. We cannot let that happen. While taxing the hell out of the rich might feel good—it might be politically popular and even have some small benefit—it will not permanently fix wealth disparity. Certainly, there are debates to be had—minimum wage and healthcare access are a couple of good examples, just for starters. There are some even harder conversations ahead of us, and employee ownership needs a seat at the table where solutions gather.

Has there ever been a better time to apply a proven formula for economic success than now? Employee ownership is the change agent that can work, not only for economic recovery, but for economic justice in America.

Hi, I'm from the Government and I'm Here to Help You!

If we can but prevent the government from wasting the labours of the people, under the pretence of taking care of them, they must become happy.[7]
—President Thomas Jefferson

Thomas Jefferson's quote from 1802 still stings today. But employee owners and employee-owned companies have never perceived the role of the American federal government as endorsing the very practice Jefferson warned us about.

And just to make sure there's no waffling on that, the ESOP Association, NCEO, and ESCA are in there fighting for us every day. The issues at the fore for ESOPs today include:

- Encouraging multigenerational private companies to consider an employee-ownership future
- Discouraging federal legislators from thinking too short term regarding tax policy

- Seeing employee ownership as a key feature to the debate about economic justice and income equality
- Holding ESOP fiduciaries accountable to their duties but not over-regulating their path to compliance

From what I've seen, both dominant political parties in America just seem to constantly want to spend more of our money. The only difference between the two widening sides is what they would actually spend it on. With America staring down the freight train of baby boomers entering retirement—*and expecting their full benefits*—this country needs to do everything in its power to help ESOPs prosper. In fact, I would argue that ESOPs can be as big a part of the long-term solution as our country wants (and allows) them to be. Finding just a small additional piece of Washington's trillions in corporate incentive pools every four to five years would make a monumental difference.

> ESOPs can be as big a part of the long-term solution as our country wants (and allows) them to be.

Dear President Biden:

Do you want to outcompete China, Russia, and other nations, whether friend or foe? Without any doubt, an expansion of employee ownership would make America more competitive. The empirical research and ground-level experiences have shown over and over again that employee-owned firms will outpace their competition, whether American or foreign. To me, when Thomas Jefferson wrote "the labours of the people," he was clearly talking about the work of early American landowners. But today, Mr. President, it is time to let loose another 14 million American employee owners, maybe even more, into the winning *owners work harder* strategy.

Anxiously awaiting your reply,
Greg Graves

P.S. And don't forget, we won't just outcompete other nations; we will build a more just economic society.

Doing Good

America is Great because she is Good.
—Alexis de Tocqueville (attributed)

Alexis de Tocqueville was a French political thinker and historian most famous for writing *Democracy in America*. In it, he described Americans as the most generous people he had ever encountered. In fact, the United Way's "Tocqueville Society" (Deanna and I are proud members) is named in honor of this all-American value. What's fascinating about de Tocqueville's take on philanthropy is how he considered this characteristic as *unique* to being an American.[8]

What was true in the 1831 of his arrival to America is true today. In all, 87 percent of American consumers say they will purchase from companies that support what they care about. Ninety-four percent of millennials say that they want their skills to benefit a cause, and sustainable investing has grown eighteenfold since 1995.[9]

Here's the amazing connection to American enterprise: Employee ownership is the greatest gift an organization can give to its employees. I've never met a successful, "Level 5" CEO who didn't give credit first and foremost to his or her people. So, it's about time to give them everything—including the firm itself. It's the gift—and the business model—that keeps giving.

> The thing is, although there may be exceptions, most people don't view working here as just a job.
>
> *—Michelle Word, Burns & McDonnell Diversity Advocate*

Single proprietor owners in America face certain technical challenges when it comes to philanthropy. It begins with the problem of having no designated price or valuation of their shares. This makes it extremely difficult for successful entrepreneurs to be philanthropic with often highly appreciated shares of the firm they own. Even a small ESOP component solves that problem by creating an annually designated value.

And when it's time for your firm to really, perhaps explosively, *do good*, I simply cannot describe to you the level that employee owners will go to help the communities where they live. Philanthropy is an inherent value for social responsibility in your people—these employee owners—that increases along with the value of their ownership accounts over time. After their *Whoa,* they will give their time and treasure at a level you cannot currently imagine.

> There's always been a sense of *What can you give back?* We all know we are so blessed by the success . . . we're very fortunate.
>
> —*Carl Weilert, principal and former employee owner,*
> *Burns & McDonnell*

The American people are born to give, and ESOPs create the perfect way for that inclination to be fully realized. When I said earlier it's okay to be proud of where you work, this is one of the best reasons ESOPs can make it so.

Condoleezza and Merrie Would Be Friends

> **The essence of America—that which really unites us—**
> **is not ethnicity or nationality or religion—it is an**
> **idea—and what an idea it is: That you can come from**
> **humble circumstances and do great things.[10]**
> —*Former U.S. secretary of state Dr. Condoleezza Rice*

In the midst of America's darkest story, Condoleezza Rice's great-great-grandmother Zina bore five children by five different slave owners. Five generations later, Rice still had to grow up in a racially segregated neighborhood in Birmingham, Alabama.[11] Let's be honest about it: Black Lives Did Not Matter. Tough odds. But she did not accept her circumstances as a barrier. She worked incredibly hard, and in 2005 she was named the first female African American secretary of state in our nation's history. She provided a role model for every little girl, black or white, in America. Not bad, Madame Secretary, not bad.

Remember Burns & Mac's Merrie? From humble, rural, working-class beginnings, Merrie entered the workforce. Without a trace of entitlement, she was hoping for, but perhaps not expecting, economic justice. But Merrie took her chance, too. She worked incredibly hard and eventually became a Top 100 shareholder in our ESOP. And I can tell you for a fact, she was a role model for every other employee owner in our firm. It was her work combined with the multiplying power of the ESOP that made her success story possible. For me, she proved what employee ownership can do for nearly any American worker.

I think Condoleezza Rice and Merrie would be friends. Their lives are stories of leveraging one's circumstances to the greatest possible advantage . . . and, in the end, doing the most good. Dr. Rice's accomplishments are, of course, groundbreaking and historical. Considering the challenges she faced, Dr. Rice's success is one in a million. But, in contrast, Merrie's success can be duplicated many million more times.

> What Dr. Rice would most appreciate, I'm certain, is that no demographic in America suffers from economic injustice more than African American women, and no group would benefit more from the encouragement and potential of employee ownership.

What Dr. Rice would most appreciate, I'm certain, is that no demographic in America suffers from economic injustice more than African American women, and no group would benefit more from the encouragement and potential of employee ownership.

To underscore the point, consider a 2019 Rutgers study that reviewed twenty-one companies across sixteen states with employment ranging from 75 to 18,000 people. Its premise was to evaluate not just whether ESOPs could help poor and moderate-income Americans build wealth (a long-established, evidence-based fact) but whether or not ESOPs could play a pivotal role in helping close wealth disparity among specific groups.

Here's what they found: African American women at companies with ESOPs had an average of *more than 275 times* the accumulated wealth of African American women nationally.[12]

No, I don't believe ESOPs are a panacea for racism or sexism in America. We have a long way to go in that regard. But they are a tool, one that should be maximized.

America Was Built for This

America was not built on fear, America was built on courage, on imagination, and on an unbeatable determination to do the job at hand.[13]
—President Harry Truman

Courage, imagination, and determination are not exclusively American qualities, but "to do the job at hand" just might be. This will be especially true as you create the ownership culture within your firm.

If employees have faith in you as their leader—real, deep, proven faith—and you ask them to knock down a wall by running head first into it (right behind you who's running into it first, that is), well, that wall is coming down. I was fortunate enough to lead Burns & Mac during a time of significant expansion. We grew, and we grew fast. I've lost track of the number of times I would personally ask a group of our employee owners to leave the "Class A" space of our world headquarters and move "temporarily" to something less accommodating until we found more room, *and* to do it over a weekend so it wouldn't affect our projects. The answer was always yes—100 percent yes.

Can you even imagine the difference in "getting the job done" between "owners" and "workers" when most of America was sent home in early 2020? I can. Moreover, how this looked for those who were "essential" and still came to work. Heroes all, but I'll still put my faith in the owner—better yet, the American owner who proved the truth of President Truman's words.

Don't forget: Growth for growth's sake is about somebody's ego trip and has nothing to do with doing the job at hand. The job at hand is to *create amazing*. Doing whatever it takes to get the job done—this "unbeatable determination"—is truly a uniquely American trait.

Especially in America

Only in America
Dreaming in red, white, and blue
Only in America
Where we dream as big as we want to
We all get a chance
Everybody gets to dance
Only in America

—Brooks & Dunn

As I sit here in 2021, there are nearly seven thousand ESOP firms in America employing more than fourteen million Americans. Only about one-third of them are 100 percent employee owned. That represents a mere 2 to 3 percent of all Americans in the workforce today.

The opportunity for explosive results is here. The chance for America to do better is here. Economic justice may not be close, but our path is crystal clear.

It's time to do better.

It's time not only to do good, but to be *great*.

WHY? Because you know that while our nation was founded chiefly on the ideal of a free society, its economic might and advantage were built on the inherent reality that "landowners" (nowadays read: *all* owners) will out-engage, out-innovate, and, in every conceivable way, out-perform their non-owner competitors. Because America's retirement challenge is upon us . . . because American exceptionalism needs a booster shot . . . and because economic justice should no longer wait.

It's time not only to do good, but to be *great*.

WHAT? The American Employee Stock Ownership Plan—thank you, Dr. Louis Kelso and Senator Russell Long—allows the workers of any firm, private or public, to share in the opportunity for wealth creation both through the contribution of their labor *and* through capital investment from future earnings by considering them owners. American ESOPs are made up of both very small and mega U.S. companies and occur across a multitude of industries. While there are some employers who are not conducive, the potential employee ownership pool is nearly one hundred million Americans.

WHO? The very best employee owners are not followers. They are believers. They are collaborators not caring who gets the credit. They are financially responsible yet motivated. They have high expectations for their boss, for their firm, and for themselves. They think in the long run. They hustle and are customer-focused. They are a diverse representation of the American melting pot. They are proud of where they work. They are ready for accelerated leadership in a world of exponentially faster growth.

HOW?

- By going 100 percent
- By getting to *Whoa!* as fast as possible
- By using financial diversity tools to de-risk
- By hiring "owners"
- By communicating with your people like the shareholders they are
- By treating employees like the owners they are
- By paying for performance
- By promoting from within 99.99 percent of the time
- By being the very best fiduciary possible
- By surrounding yourself with the right board, legal team, and trustee experts
- By being the very best place to work

The ESOP opportunity is exceptionally American: American in terms of the given opportunity for both success and treasure, but also and predominantly because it creates the best opportunity to move America forward as an economically just nation.

It is time to do this . . . it's time to *wake up the American Dream.*

ACKNOWLEDGMENTS

My thanks go, first and last, to the employee owners of Burns & McDonnell. You believed in me, tolerated me, and worked beyond imagination for me. You took our firm from good, to great, to even greater still. You work like owners every day, not just for the annual meeting or on Chili Bowl Day. You act like owners when the client calls you at midnight, when your fellow owner needs a last-minute assist, and when your community reaches out for help. You take more pride in our firm's "good" than in its "wealth." I've never met a more giving people, of both time and treasure. I miss writing you every Friday. What I miss even more is how so many of you would always write me back with a note of love and encouragement. I love you back.

Thank you, Melissa, Ali, and John, for putting into words how it felt to *create amazing*.

Thank you, Lee Orrison, for the graphics, and Lance Warren, for the photos.

Thank you to my coauthor and editor, Leeanne Seaver. I met Leeanne while she was penning the University of Kansas Health System turnaround story. She is very good at what she does. She's a wordsmith and collaborator, tough as to her standards of quality and integrity, but also consistently patient and encouraging of me. Hiring Leeanne was my best editorial decision. She shepherded me to the end.

Thank you to my author/hero, Jim Collins. In just a few emails, two personal meetings, and a one-hour phone call, he shaped my belief system and through it, this book. That one-hour call also led to another one thousand or so hours of work by me! He was, as usual, right.

Thank you to my Critical Thinking Group for your review, for letting me bug you, for your honesty, and for a couple of the best ideas: Doug Criner, Denny Scott, Melissa Lavin, Bob Grossman, Mariner Kemper, Stephen Smith, Dr. Joseph Blasi, Stephanie Silverman, Ali Mahaffy, and Steve Gross.

Thank you to my agent and newest good friend, John Willig, a terrific mentor and ever patient with me. You talked me away from several cliffs.

Thank you to Matt Holt, Leah Wilson, and the entire team at BenBella. I simply cannot describe how much better this book is thanks to you.

Thank you, Mel. I believe you would have been proud to hold this book in your hands. I miss you indescribably.

Thank you, Jessica, Jason, Kristin, Ford, Greg, and Alyssa. A prouder dad there never was.

Thank you, Deuce, Cooper, Max, Gabe, Ellie Grace, Baby Ford, and, I hope, many more to come. Gramps loves you unconditionally.

APPENDIX: THE BURNS & MCDONNELL TIMELINE

It's always amazing for me to revisit the Burns & Mac journey from its humble beginnings. I'm grateful to Lance Warren, the company's official historian, for help in compiling the information that follows.

1898
Burns & McDonnell Engineering Company moves into the New England Life Building in downtown Kanas City, Missouri. Its office is 100 square feet large and has no telephone.

1899
Both Burns and McDonnell take jobs with the Kansas City Park Board just to help pay the rent.

1899
McDonnell wins Burns & McDonnell's first assignment: a drinking water and streetlight power project for the small town of Iola, Kansas. Iola would remain a faithful client for more than 100 years.

1905
Employee Head Count = 5.

1915
Employee Head Count = 20.

1924
Clinton Burns dies of throat cancer on April 1, twenty-six years to the day after he and McDonnell had started the firm.

1928
McDonnell is selected by the Board of Water and Power Commissioners of Los Angeles as a member of a board of three engineers to study and report on a ten-year program of water improvements for the City of Los Angeles. This appointment is made as a result of the St. Francis Dam disaster in San Francisquito Canyon, California, in which more than 432 people died. McDonnell is also part of a group of six advisory engineers tasked with studying the location and laying out Boulder Dam, which, in 1947, would be renamed the Hoover Dam.

1933
Employee Head Count = 42.

1935
President Franklin D. Roosevelt proposes the Rural Electrification Act. Although the firm has done only a bit of power distribution in its past, this is the first catalyst to create what would eventually become the firm's largest division.

1940
Emplyee Head Count = 43.

1941-1945
America is engaged in World War II. Burns & McDonnell provide architectural and engineering expertise with some seven hundred employees

supporting twenty-two different military projects throughout the Midwest, including Smoky Hill Air Base in Salina, Kansas; Rosecrans Air Field in St. Joseph, Missouri; Herrington Army Airfield in Herrington, Kansas; and the Army Air Force Supply Depot in Topeka, Kansas.

1948

Burns & McDonnell Engineering Company turns fifty years old. It has worked on projects in 854 American cities and 44 states.

1951

Robert E. McDonnell semi-retires.

1951

R. H. McDonnell becomes the managing partner of Burns & McDonnell. Employee Head Count = 88.

1960

Founder R. E. McDonnell dies at the age of eighty-seven.

1961

Employee Head Count = 221.

1962

President John F. Kennedy attends the dedication of America's first airport designed specifically for jet aircraft: Dulles International Airport in Washington, D.C. Burns & McDonnell worked on the master planning, design, and construction management for the project. Later, the firm is commissioned to do the lighting design for President Kennedy's gravesite.

1964

The U.S. Naval Station in San Juan, Puerto Rico, selects Burns & McDonnell to investigate the quality of electric power and transmission systems for the U.S. Naval base in Guantanamo Bay, Cuba.

1965

Burns & McDonnell is selected to do master planning, partial design, and construction supervision for the new Kansas City International Airport.

1970

Employee Head Count = 381.

1971

R. H. McDonnell sells the firm to Armco Steel. *Ugh.*

1972

The Kansas City International Airport, a now 6,000-square-foot, $250,000,000 project, opens with the now-famous "Drive to Your Gate" design. The next year it is named "One of Ten Outstanding Engineering Achievements" by the National Society of Professional Engineers.

1974

R. H. McDonnell retires.

1974

Ray Luhnow becomes president of Burns & McDonnell.

Employee Head Count = 544.

ERISA legislation is passed in Washington and, among many other actions, creates the legal tax structure for an ESOP.

1977

After assisting in the site selection across five states, construction begins on what is easily the firm's largest project in its history to date: the Laramie River Power Station. Even today, it is one of the lowest-cost energy producers in America.

1979

Merrie Barnett (soon-to-be Ferguson) begins entry-level graphics work at Burns & Mac for $4 an hour.

1980

Needing talent to meet the growing demand for its services, Burns & McDonnell's recruiting efforts reach as far as small-school, small-town South Dakota, where they find me. It is the fall of 1979; I am newly married and in my last year at the South Dakota School of Mines and Technology. Although Kansas City isn't even on my radar, there is simply something about that firm that keeps bringing me back to their offer. For one, I love the diversity of the work and how quickly they promised to literally dump responsibility on me. My bride, Deanna, is on board, so I sign on for $18,000 per year. We load up the Chevy Nova and head south. It's a good thing I don't know what would happen to the company next (and an even better thing that I survive it).

Employee Head Count = 1,346.

My first day of Burns & Mac employment: June 30.

Bob McDonnell dies at the age of seventy-five.

1981

Less than a year after my start at the company, the firm loses more than half its backlog with two large power plant project cancellations. Massive layoffs occur and a voluntary reduced workweek (that was anything but voluntary) is instituted. Employment plummets from a record high of almost 1,400 to nearly 800, eventually bottoming out around 600 a few years later. Somehow (thank you, Joel), I survive.

1982

Ray Luhnow retires.

Newt Campbell becomes the president of Burns & McDonnell.

1983

Prompted by the Clean Air Act, the firm's Air Quality Division lands a mega air pollution control project for Louisville Gas & Electric. Employment is still dropping, but more slowly and mostly from attrition. A young engineer by the name of Greg Graves and his wife take deep sighs of relief.

With the acquisition of C.W. Nofsinger Company, a firm specializing in chemical processing plants, Burns & McDonnell cultivates what will become, over time, the firm's mega OG&C Division (Oil, Gas & Chemicals).

1984

Newt Campbell is promoted by Armco to president of its Professional Services Division. Dave Ruf becomes the fifth president of Burns & McDonnell.

1985

May: Armco officially announces it will be selling its Professional Services Division—including Burns & McDonnell.

June: Newt Campbell and others meet with Philadelphia-based management consultants from The Coxe Group. They recommend the idea of forming Burns & Mac as an ESOP.

July: Newt Campbell and Dave Ruf begin regular, all-employee meetings announcing the idea and their support for a 100 percent ESOP buyout.

July: The firm brings in ESOP-ERISA, legal, tax, banking, and acquisition consultants.

August: After nail-biting negotiations, Armco elects to decline a higher bid from German diesel manufacturer Klöckner-Humboldt-Deutz and allows the employees of Burns & McDonnell to buy the firm. Details of the negotiations continue through December. The firm agrees to a five-year payout of a percent of its profits back to Armco to sweeten the deal. The purchase price is confidential, but taking all factors into account, it's about 30 percent of what the firm was purchased for originally by Armco.

1986

One hundred percent employee ownership begins January 1.

Employee Head Count = 611.

Newt Campbell returns to Burns & McDonnell as chairman and CEO.

Dave Ruf remains president.

1988

Burns & McDonnell lands its largest international project in the firm's history to date. Working with the U.S. Corps of Engineers, Burns & Mac provides the complete design services for the Amoun Air Base in Egypt, a project that dates back to the 1978 Camp David Accord in which peace agreements facilitated by President Jimmy Carter were signed by Egyptian president Anwar Sadat and Israeli prime minister Menachem Begin.

1990

Employee Head Count = 926.

1993

The final ESOP loan payment is made to UMB Bank on December 31. The firm is debt-free, and it never looks back.

1994

On January 3, Newt Campbell and Dave Ruf, along with UMB banker R. Crosby Kemper Jr., convene all employees in the courtyard to burn the mortgage on the loan, followed by a chili feast outside. The event is dubbed the firm's *Chili Bowl* and is still celebrated on the first working day of each new year.

Newt Campbell retires.

Dave Ruf becomes CEO and Chairman.

Burns & McDonnell now has regional offices in Denver, Miami, Dallas, St. Louis, and Singapore.

1995

Don Greenwood is hired, and the firm's Construction Services Division becomes the firm's Construction/Design-Build Division. Financial success booms.

Employee Head Count = 1,132.

Burns & McDonnell headquarters moves to 9400 Ward Parkway, still in Kansas City but for the first time ever into Class A office space.

1997

A University of Washington State Business School study finds that members of ESOPs had retirement savings *three times* that of comparable non-ESOP workers.

Greg Graves becomes president of the firm's Energy Division.

1998

Burns & McDonnell celebrates its one hundredth birthday.

2000

A Rutgers School of Management study concludes ESOP companies grow between 2.3 percent and 2.4 percent faster than would have been expected without it.

John Nobles is hired, and Bob McDonnell has new competition for "best salesman in the history of the firm." The firm's oil, gas, and chemical business "explodes."

Employee Head Count = 1,498.

2002

Dave Ruf announces the new president of the company and the firm's next CEO will be Greg Graves (that's me).

Burns & McDonnell changes from a C Corp to an S Corp.

Employee Head Count = 1,667.

2003

Dave Ruf retires.

2004

Graves becomes the firm's sixth CEO.

Within the first month, Graves begins on his promised list of one hundred changes to the firm, including naming Don Greenwood as its newest board member, Denny Scott as Chief Administrative Officer, Melissa

Wood as Director of Human Resources, Joel Cerwick as President (and champion) of Regional Offices, Jim Foil as General Manager of the Infrastructure Division, Greg Gould as the firm's first Chief Technical & Risk Officer, Jeff Greig as General Manager of the new Business & Technical Services Division, Melissa Lavin as the Director of the Burns & McDonnell Foundation, and future CEO Ray Kowalik as the new General Manager of the firm's Energy Division.

Graves pens the first of his 652 *Friday News* emails to every employee owner. The first begins "Safety: First in our Vision, First in our Actions . . . starting right now."

2005
Employee Head Count = 1,983.

2006
After 108 years, Burns & McDonnell reaches 2,000 employee owners. It will take only four more years to reach 3,000.

2007
Merrie Ferguson has been rising through the ranks and is now a Section Chief in Burns & McDonnell's Energy Group.

2008
Denver Office General Manager Paul Fischer is named President of Burns & McDonnell's Regional Office Group. He grows the group so successfully it will pass Kansas City's employee population within six years.

2009
Fortune magazine names Burns & McDonnell one of the 100 Best Companies to Work For in America, coming in at number 50.

2010
Greg and Deanna Graves are named Kansas City's *Philanthropists of the Year.*

Employee Head Count = 3,043.

2011

Burns & McDonnell celebrates twenty-five years of employee ownership. Greg hosts a company-wide party to celebrate. All ten members of The Big 10 are present.

2012

Burns & McDonnell is named the *ESOP Company of the Year* by the ESOP Association.

Firm opens its record thirty-second regional office in Calgary, Alberta.

Fortune magazine elevates Burns & Mac to number 26 on its 100 Best Companies to Work For in America list.

2013

Graves announces the promotion of Mike Brown to the new position of CEO, Burns & McDonnell International. The firm opens offices in Mumbai, India, with the acquisition of Chemtex, including 260 employees. In 2019, the Mumbai office reaches nearly 750 employees.

Employee Head Count = 4,392.

2014

Sales exceed $2.5 billion.

Fortune ranks Burns & Mac at number 14!

Professional Services Management Journal awards Burns & McDonnell its Premier Award for Client Satisfaction.

Employee Head Count = 5,040.

2015

Led by future-CEO Ray Kowalik, the firm begins the acquisition of direct-hire and employee-owned construction firm AZCO out of Appleton, Wisconsin, and another new era begins.

Kansas City Business Journal names Burns & McDonnell the best place to work in Kansas City for the third consecutive year.

At age fifty-eight, Merrie Ferguson retires to her dream home on Lake of the Ozarks.

2016

Graves announces his retirement at the end of the year. One week later, by unanimous vote of the board of directors, he announces that Ray Kowalik will become the firm's new CEO at the beginning of 2017.

Employee Head Count = 6,065.

2017

Ray Kowalik becomes the firm's seventh CEO.

Sales exceed $3 billion.

2018

Burns & McDonnell makes second acquisition into direct-hire construction with Ref-Chem, a non-union contractor out of Baton Rouge, Louisiana.

Employee Head Count = 6,709.

2019

Expansion of the World Headquarters offices begins . . . again.

Total sales exceed $4 billion.

2020

Burns & McDonnell sends the vast majority of its employee owners home in early March to "work from home" during the COVID-19 pandemic.

The Perfect Gentleman, Ray Luhnow, dies at ninety-seven.

ENDNOTES

Introduction

1. Blasi, Joseph, Richard B. Freeman, and Douglas Kruse. *The Citizen's Share: Putting Ownership Back into Democracy.* New Haven, CT: Yale University Press, 2013.
2. Case, John. "An Economy in Waiting: Fighting Inequality by Turning Workers into Owners." *The New Republic,* July 8, 2019. https://newrepublic.com/article/154107/economy-waiting.
3. Blasi, Joseph, and Douglas L. Kruse. "Business Owners Have New Incentive to Sell to Their Workers." *Finance & Commerce,* August 15, 2018. https://finance-commerce.com/2018/08/business-owners-have-new-incentive-to-sell-to-their-workers/.
4. Case, "An Economy in Waiting."
5. General Social Survey 2014 and 2018 funded by The Employee Ownership Foundation, The National Opinion Research Center at the University of Chicago. Analytics by Kruse and Blasi (2019).
6. Blasi, Freeman, and Kruse, *The Citizen's Share*
7. Ibid.
8. Ibid.

Chapter One

1. Blasi, Joseph, Richard B. Freeman, and Douglas Kruse. *The Citizen's Share: Putting Ownership Back into Democracy*. New Haven, CT: Yale University Press, 2013.
2. Interview with Leeanne Seaver, May 2019.
3. Interview with Leeanne Seaver, April 2019.

Chapter Two

1. "Thoughts on the Business of Life." *Forbes*, September 29, 2005. www.forbes.com/global/2005/1010/088A.html?sh=3a34df724695.
2. Blasi, Joseph, Richard B. Freeman, and Douglas Kruse. *The Citizen's Share: Putting Ownership Back into Democracy*. New Haven, CT: Yale University Press, 2013.
3. Buchele, Robert, Douglas Kruse, Loren Rodgers, and Adria Scharf. "Show Me the Money: Does Shared Capitalism Share the Wealth?" The National Bureau of Economic Research, April 2009. www.nber.org/papers/w14830.
4. Collins, Jim. *Good to Great*. New York City: HarperCollins Publishers, 2001.
5. Ibid.
6. Ibid.
7. Ibid.
8. Interview with Greg Graves, July 2019.
9. Dewar, Carolyn, Scott Keller, Kevin Sneader, and Kurt Strovink. "The CEO Moment: Leadership for a New Era." *McKinsey Quarterly*, July 21, 2020. www.mckinsey.com/featured-insights/leadership/the-ceo-moment-leadership-for-a-new-era.
10. "The 100 Best Companies to Work For." *Fortune*, February 2, 2009. https://archive.fortune.com/magazines/fortune/bestcompanies/2009/full_list/.
11. Buchele, et al. "Show Me the Money."
12. Blasi, Joseph, Richard B. Freeman, and Douglas L. Kruse. "Evidence: What the U.S. Research Shows About Worker Ownership." In Oxford University Press Handbook of Mutual, Co-Operative and Co-Owned Business. Oxford, United Kingdom: Oxford University Press, 2017. https://dash.harvard.edu/bitstream/handle/1/34591608/Evidence_What_the_Research_Shows__MS-final_Blasi-Freemann-Kruse_OUP-Hdbk_2016.pdf?sequence=4.
13. Rosen, Corey. *Employee Ownership Blog*, July 31, 2020. https://www.nceo.org/employee-ownership-blog/companies-espps-outperform-those-without-them.
14. Lipsit, Seymour Martin. *The First New Nation: The United States in Historical and Comparative Perspective*. New York City: Doubleday Anchor Books, 1967.
15. "The Gettysburg Address," Abraham Lincoln online, accessed December 8, 2020. http://www.abrahamlincolnonline.org/lincoln/speeches/gettysburg.htm.
16. Reich, Robert. "When Bosses Shared Their Profits." *New York Times*, June 25, 2020. www.nytimes.com/2020/06/25/opinion/sunday/corporate-profit-sharing-inequality.html.

17. Ashford, Robert. "Binary Economics: An Overview." Syracuse University College of Law, 2010. https://surface.syr.edu/lawpub/15.

18. "Policy Basics: Top Ten Facts About Social Security." Center on Budget and Policy Basics, accessed August 14, 2019. www.cbpp.org/research/social -security/policy-basics-top-ten-facts-about-social-security.

19. Hoyt, Jeff. "Senior Living History: 1930–1939." SeniorLiving.org, April 19, 2018. www.seniorliving.org/history/1930-1939/.

20. Amsted Industries Home Page, accessed November 5, 2020. www.amsted .com/.

21. "100 Best Companies to Work For 2016." *Fortune,* accessed December 4, 2020. https://fortune.com/best-companies/2016/publix-super-markets.

22. Calhoun, Amy. "Gore Marks 20th Year on 100 Best Companies to Work For® List." Gore News & Events, March 9, 2017. www.gore.com/news-events /press-release/enterprise-press-release-fortune-100-list-2017-us.

23. Billock, Jennifer. "Southwest Employees Receive Record Breaking $620 Million in Profit Sharing." FlyerTalk.com, February 12. 2016. www.flyertalk .com/articles/southwest-employees-receive-record-breaking-620-million-in -proft-sharing.html.

24. Mueller, Heather. "An Inspiring Example of Employee Ownership (Interview with Steel Encounters)." Emplify.com, accessed December 4, 2020. https://emplify.com/blog/steel-encounters/.

25. Tims, Dana. "Founder of Bob's Red Mill Natural Foods Transfers Business to Employees." *Oregonian*, February 17, 2010. www.oregonlive.com /clackamascounty/2010/02/bobs_red_mill_natural_foods_ro.html.

26. Josephs, Mary. "Millionaire Grocery Clerks: The Amazing WinCo Food Story." *Forbes*, November 5, 2014. www.forbes.com/sites/maryjosephs/2014/11/05 /millionaire-grocery-clerks-the-amazing-winco-foods-story/#2b67e4d05700.

Chapter Three

1. Interview with Greg Graves. August 8, 2019.

2. Bob's Red Mill Home Page, accessed December 4, 2020. www.bobsredmill .com.

3. "Employee Stock Ownership Plan (ESOP) Facts." National Center for Employee Ownership (NCEO), accessed December 4, 2020. www.esop.org.

4. "How Louis Kelso Invented the ESOP." Employee-Owned America, accessed December 4, 2020; and The Kelso Institute, accessed December 4, 2020. http://kelsoinstitute.org/louiskelso/.

5. Menke, John, and Dickson Buxton. "The Origin and History of the ESOP and Its Future Role as a Business Succession Tool." *Journal of Financial Service Professionals*, May 2010. www.menke.com/archives_articles/origin -history-of-esops.pdf.

6. Reich, Robert. "When Bosses Shared Their Profits." *New York Times*, June 25, 2020. www.nytimes.com/2020/06/25/opinion/sunday/corporate-profit -sharing-inequality.html.

7. Interview with Leeanne Seaver, July 2020.

8. "The Life of Louis Kelso: Father of the ESOP." *Hardy Blog*, October 31, 2019. http://blog.hardydiagnostics.com/2019/10/the-life-of-louis-kelso-father-of-the-esop/.

9. Menke and Buxton, "The Origin and History of the ESOP."

10. Menke and Buxton, "The Origin and History of the ESOP"; "How Louis Kelso Invented the ESOP."

11. Menke and Buxton, "The Origin and History of the ESOP."

12. Menke and Buxton, "The Origin and History of the ESOP"; and "How Louis Kelso Invented the ESOP."

13. Martin, Michael S. *Russell Long: A Life in Politics*. Jackson, MS: University Press of Mississippi, 2014.

14. Ibid.

15. Menke and Buxton, "The Origin and History of the ESOP."

16. Ibid.

17. Rosen, Corey. "Rewind to the 1970s TV Interview with Louis Kelso, the Father of ESOPs." *Employee Ownership Blog*. National Center for Employee Ownership, October 3, 2019. www.nceo.org/article/rewind-1970s-tv-interview-louis-kelso-father-esops.

18. "HB17-1214: Encourage Employee Ownership of Existing Small Business," Colorado General Assembly, accessed December 4, 2020. http://leg.colorado.gov/bills/hb17-1214.

19. "Bill to Expand Employee-Ownership Passed into Law Through Veto Override." Missouri Chamber of Commerce and Industry, September 15, 2016. www.mochamber.com/news/esop_passed_into_law.

20. Rodgers, Loren. "Reaction to Iowa Governor's ESOP Initiative." *Employee Ownership Blog*. National Center for Employee Ownership, February 15, 2012. https://www.nceo.org/blog/reaction-iowa-governors-esop-initiative.

21. "Worker-Owned Recovery California," Sustainable Economies Law Center, accessed December 4, 2020. https://www.theselc.org/worc_coalition.

22. "The Employee Ownership 100: America's Largest Majority Employee-Owned Companies." *Employee Ownership Blog*. National Center for Employee Ownership, July 27, 2020. www.nceo.org/articles/employee-ownership-100.

23. Interview with Greg Graves. August 5, 2019.

24. Jeffrey, Terrence P. "21,995,000 to 12,329,000: Government Employees Outnumber Manufacturing Employees 1.8 to 1." CNSNews.com, September 8, 2015. www.cnsnews.com/news/article/terence-p-jeffrey/21955000-12329000-government-employees-outnumber-manufacturing.

25. "Nonprofits Account for 11.4 Million Jobs, 10.3 Percent of All Private Sector Employment." *Economics Daily*, Bureau of Labor Statistics, U.S. Department of Labor, October 21, 2014. www.bls.gov/opub/ted/2014/ted_20141021.htm.

26. "Alphabet Market Cap 2006–2019 | GOOGL." Macrotrends.com, accessed July 2020. www.macrotrends.net/stocks/charts/GOOGL/alphabet/market-cap.

27. Hess, Alexander. "The 10 Largest Employers in America." *USA Today*, August 22, 2013. www.usatoday.com/story/money/business/2013/08/22/ten -largest-employers/2680249/.

28. Duffin, Erin. "Full-Time Employees—Unadjusted Monthly Number in the U.S." Statista.com, accessed July 2020. www.statista.com/statistics/192361 /unadjusted-monthly-number-of-full-time-employees-in-the-us/.

29. Case, John. "An Economy in Waiting: Fighting Inequality by Turning Workers into Owners." *New Republic*, July 8, 2019. https://newrepublic.com /article/154107/economy-waiting.

30. Weltman, Barbara. "Employee Stock Ownership Plans Are a Win-Win." Big Ideas for Small Business, February 20, 2020. https://bigideasforsmall business.com/employee-stock-ownership-plans-are-a-win-win/.

31. Interview with Greg Graves. August 2019.

32. Blasi, Joseph, Richard B. Freeman, and Douglas Kruse. *The Citizen's Share: Putting Ownership Back into Democracy*. New Haven, CT: Yale University Press, 2013.

33. Menke and Buxton, "The Origin and History of the ESOP."

34. Menke and Buxton, "The Origin and History of the ESOP"; and "How Louis Kelso Invented the ESOP."

35. "S&P 500." S&P Dow Jones Indices, accessed July 2020. www.spglobal .com/spdji/en/indices/equity/sp-500/#overview.

36. "What Is a Worker Cooperative?" Democracy at Work Institute, U.S. Federation of Worker Cooperatives, accessed July 2020. https://institute.coop/ what-worker-cooperative.

37. "What Are Fiduciaries, What Are Their Responsibilities, and How Do They Get Appointed?" ESOP Strategies/SES ESOP Services, accessed December 5, 2020. https://sesesop.com/esop-knowledge-center/esop-legal/esop-fiduciaries -responsibilities-get-appointed/.

38. Ibid.

39. "ESOP Trustees," ESOPTrustee.co, accessed July 2020. www.esoptrustee.co.

40. "ESOPS in Your State," Employee-Owned S Corporations of America (ESCA), accessed December 2020. www.esca.us.

41. Brill, Alex. "Employee Stock Ownership Plans as an Exit Strategy for Private Business Owners." Matrix Global Advisors, March 2017. http://getmga.com /wp-content/uploads/2017/04/ESCA_ExitStrategy_Final.pdf.

42. Silverman, Stephanie. Stephanie Silverman to Senator Mike Crapo and Senator Sherrod Brown, April 6, 2015. http://esca.us/wp-content /uploads/2015/11/ESCA_statement_submitted_to_Savings_and_Investment _Working_Group_April_6_2015.pdf.

43. "About the ESOP Association." The ESOP Association, accessed December 4, 2020. www.esopassociation.org/about.

44. Ibid.

45. "Learn More About Employee-Owned S Corporations of America (ESCA)." Employee-Owned S Corporations of America, accessed December 5, 2020. https://esca.us/about-us/about-esca/.

46. National Center for Employee Ownership, accessed December 5, 2020. www.nceo.org/about.

47. "Institute for the Study of Employee Ownership and Profit Sharing." Rutgers School of Management and Labor Relations, accessed December 5, 2020. https://smlr.rutgers.edu/content/institute-study-employee-ownership -and-profit-sharing.

48. Joffe, David, and John Titus. "Sarbanes-Oxley: What It Means for Private Companies and ESOPs." *Journal of Employee Ownership Law and Finance*, March 15, 2004.

49. "S.2786: Main Street Employee Ownership Act of 2018." 115th Congress (2017–2018). www.congress.gov/bill/115th-congress/senate-bill/2786.

50. Blasi, Joseph, and Douglas L. Kruse. "Business Owners Have New Incentive to Sell to Their Workers." *Finance & Commerce*, August 15, 2018. https:// finance-commerce.com/2018/08/business-owners-have-new-incentive-to-sell -to-their-workers/.

Chapter Four

1. Medintz, Scott. "The 25 Most Influential Business Management Books." *Time*, August 9, 2011.

2. Interview with Leeanne Seaver. June 2020.

3. Bariso, Justin. "Mark Cuban: Want Your Business to Survive? Make Your Employees Owners." *Inc.*, May 13, 2020. www.inc.com/justin-bariso/mark -cuban-employees-ownership-linkedin.html.

4. Rodgers, Loren. "In Response to COVID-19: What Employee-Owners Are Doing." *Employee Ownership Blog*. National Center for Employee Ownership, April 15, 2020. www.nceo.org/employee-ownership-blog/response -covid-19-what-employee-owners-are-doing.

5. Miller, Todd. "Our ESOP Is the Ultimate Unifier." Employee-Owned S Corporations of America, January 29, 2019. esca.us/2019/01/the-ultimate -unifier.

6. "Employees Love ESOPs—and Research Proves It." *ESOP Association Blog*. The ESOP Association, October 1, 2020. esopassociation.org/articles /employees-love-esops-and-research-proves-it.

7. *Employee Ownership & Economic Well-Being*. National Center for Employee Ownership, May 15, 2017. www.ownershipeconomy.org/wp-content/uploads /2017/05/employee_ownership_and_economic_wellbeing_2017.pdf.

8. Interview with Leeanne Seaver. June 2020.

9. WinCo Foods, accessed December 5, 2020. https://careers.wincofoods.com.

10. "Committed to Diversity." Publix.com, accessed December 5, 2020. corporate.publix.com/about-publix/culture/committed-to-diversity.

11. Interview with Leeanne Seaver. June 2020.

12. Interview with Greg Graves. June 2020.

13. Interview with Leeanne Seaver. July 2020.

Chapter Five

1. Blasi, Joseph, Richard B. Freeman, and Douglas Kruse. *The Citizen's Share*: *Putting Ownership Back into Democracy*. New Haven, CT: Yale University Press, 2013.
2. Kruse, Douglas, Joseph Blasi, and Richard Freeman. "Does Linking Worker Pay to Firm Performance Help the Best Firms Do Even Better?" National Bureau of Economic Research, January 2012.
3. "*Fortune* 100 Best Companies to Work For 2019." Great Place to Work, 2019. www.greatplacetowork.com/best-workplaces/100-best/2019.
4. Publix. "Publix Donates More Than 1 Million Pounds of Produce, 100,000 Gallons of Milk in First Two Weeks of Effort to Support Farmers, Feed Those in Need." PerishableNews.com, May 7, 2020. https://www .perishablenews.com/dairy/publix-donates-more-than-1-million-pounds-of -produce-100000-gallons-of-milk-in-first-two-weeks-of-effort-to-support -farmers-feed-those-in-need/.
5. Dewar, Carolyn, Scott Keller, Kevin Sneader, and Kurt Strovink. "The CEO Moment: Leadership for a New Era." *McKinsey Quarterly*, July 21, 2020. www.mckinsey.com/featured-insights/leadership/the-ceo-moment -leadership-for-a-new-era.
6. Ibid.
7. U.S. Code Title 26—INTERNAL REVENUE CODE. Legal Information Institute, Cornell Law School, accessed December 5, 2020. www.law.cornell .edu/uscode/text/26.
8. Rosen, Corey. "Companies with ESPPs Outperform Those Without Them," *Employee Ownership Blog*, July 31, 2020. https://www.nceo.org /employee-ownership-blog/companies-espps-outperform-those-without-them.
9. Shwantes, Marcel. "Why Do People Quit Their Jobs Exactly? Here's the Entire Reason, Summed Up in 1 Sentence." *Inc.*, May 30, 2017. https://www .inc.com/marcel-schwantes/why-do-people-really-quit-their-jobs-heres-the -entire-reason-summed-up-in-1-sent.html.
10. Lipman, Victor. *The Type B Manager: Leading Successfully in a Type A World*. New York City: Prentice Hall Press, 2015.
11. Schwantes, Marcel. "Why Do People Quit Their Jobs, Exactly?" *Inc.*, May 30, 2017. www.inc.com/get.inc/helping-consumers-access-financial-resources-to -build-better-lives.html.
12. Interview with Leeanne Seaver. July 2020.
13. Lundin, Stephen, Harry Paul, John Christensen, and Kenneth Blanchard. *Fish! A Remarkable Way to Boost Morale and Improve Results*. New York City: Hachette Books, 2000.

Chapter Six

1. Truslow, James. *The Epic of America*. Boston, MA: Little Brown and Company, 1931.

2. McCoy, Drew R. *The Elusive Republic: Political Economy in Jeffersonian America*. Chapel Hill, NC: The University of North Carolina Press, 1980.

3. Ibid.

4. "CESJ Initiatives and Innovations." Center for Economic and Social Justice, accessed December 5, 2020. ww.cesj.org/about-cesj-in-brief/history-accomplishments/cesj-initiatives-innovations.

5. "President Ronald Reagan's Speech on Project Economic Justice." Center for Economic and Social Justice, transcript of speech presented at the White House, Washington, D.C., August 3, 1987. www.cesj.org/about-cesj-in-brief/history-accomplishments/pres-reagans-speech-on-project-economic-justice/.

6. Fauci, Anthony. "A Goal of Service to Humankind," as heard on *All Things Considered*, July 25, 2005. thisIbelieve.org/essay/15.

7. Jefferson, Thomas. "Wasting the Labours of the People (Quotation), November 29, 1802." Thomas Jefferson Encyclopedia. Monticello.org, accessed December 5, 2020. www.monticello.org/site/research-and-collections/wasting-labours-people-quotation.

8. "The Tocqueville Society." United Way, accessed December 5, 2020. www.unitedway.org/get-involved/groups/tocqueville-society.

9. Dewar, Carolyn, Scott Keller, Kevin Sneader, and Kurt Strovink. "The CEO Moment: Leadership for a New Era." *McKinsey Quarterly*, July 21, 2020. www.mckinsey.com/featured-insights/leadership/the-ceo-moment-leadership-for-a-new-era.

10. Anderson, Amy Rees. "How to Achieve More Than the American Dream." *Forbes*, April 19, 2017. www.forbes.com/sites/amyanderson/2017/04/19/how-to-achieve-more-than-the-american-dream/#4d682cf94542.

11. Rice, Condoleeza. *Democracy: Stories from the Long Road to Freedom*. New York City: Twelve Books, 2017.

12. Blasi, Joseph, Douglas Kruse, Janet Boguslaw, and Lisa Schur. "Building the Assets of Low and Moderate Income Workers and Their Families: The Role of Employee Ownership." The Institute for the Study of Employee Ownership and Profit Sharing, Rutgers School of Management and Labor Relations, March 2019. https://smlr.rutgers.edu/sites/default/files/rutgerskellogg report_april2019.pdf.

13. "Special Message to Congress: The President's First Economic Report," Harry S. Truman Library, accessed December 8, 2020. https://www.truman library.gov/library/public-papers/4/special-message-congress-presidents-first-economic-report.

PHOTOGRAPHY CREDITS

Photos on pages 8, 13, 14, 15, 17, 21, 23 24, 25, 168: courtesy of Burns & McDonnell
Photos on pages 5, 42, 45 72, 75, 76, 77, 78, 92, 107, 159: credit, Lee Orrison and
    courtesy of Burns & McDonnell

Photos on:
page 52:   courtesy of Merrie Ferguson
page 59:   courtesy of Patricia Kelso
page 161: courtesy of Jewish Community Relations Bureau | AJC Kansas City,
           credit: Brian Turner
page 207: Ellie Grace Photography

ABOUT THE AUTHOR

As chairman and CEO of Burns & McDonnell, Greg Graves led one of the fastest-growing and most successful engineering, architecture, construction, and environmental consulting firms in North America. Graves began his career at Burns & McDonnell in 1980, fresh out of college. Twenty-two years later, at the age of forty-three, he was named just the sixth CEO in the firm's 104-year history. He became CEO on January 1, 2004. From 2004–2016, the firm flourished:

- Employment grew from 1,500 to 5,500 employee-owners . . . all organically.
- Revenues grew from $300 million to almost $3 billion.
- The average ROI to employee owners was over 25 percent.

- It was named one of *Fortune* magazine's Top 100 Best Places to Work six times, coming in 14th in 2014, and Kansas City's Best Place to Work six times in a row.
- The corporate foundation grew 1,000 percent.
- Graves was named Kansas City Philanthropist of the Year (along with his wife, Deanna Graves) in 2013, *EY*'s Entrepreneur of the Year Midwest in 2014, and Kansas Citian of the Year in 2015.

In retirement, Greg has been the chairman of the board for two iconic Kansas City metro institutions that are trailblazers in fields he is extremely passionate about—healthcare and the arts. Greg was named chair of the University of Kansas Hospital Authority Board from 2014–2020 after serving as a board member since 2009. The Kansas City Repertory Theatre also appointed Greg as chairman of its board for two years after he served on its executive committee for one year. Greg also serves on the board of Barstow School in Kansas City, and as the lead director of UMB Financial Corporation, a $30 billion bank headquartered in Kansas City.

Greg has a bachelor of science in mechanical engineering from the South Dakota School of Mines & Technology, a master of business administration from Rockhurst University, and multiple honorary doctorate recognitions.

You can find Greg online at www.greggraves.com and on Twitter at @GregMGraves.